PLUS ONE

PLUS ONE

A Year in the Life
of a Hollywood Nobody

CLAIRE FORDHAM

KENSINGTON BOOKS
http://www.kensingtonbooks.com

KENSINGTON BOOKS are published by

Kensington Publishing Corp.
850 Third Avenue
New York, NY 10022

All Kensington titles, imprints and distributed lines are available at special quantity discounts for bulk purchases for sales promotion, premiums, fund-raising, educational or institutional use.

Special book excerpts or customized printings can also be created to fit specific needs. For details, write or phone the office of the Kensington Special Sales Manager: Kensington Publishing Corp., 850 Third Avenue, New York, NY 10022. Attn. Special Sales Department. Phone: 1-800-221-2647.

Kensington and the K logo Reg. U.S. Pat & TM Off

ISBN: 0-7582-0918-5

First printing: June 2005
10 9 8 7 6 5 4 3 2 1

Printed in the United States of America

For Julia, Max, and Mia—
I am nothing without you.

ACKNOWLEDGMENTS

I am forever indebted to my sister, Julia, for lighting the beacon, for her wisdom, kindness, humor, example, and unconditional love and for inviting me to share her wonderful life in California.

My children, Max and Mia Cross, are my greatest joy. I love you and hope all your dreams come true.

Mum and Dad, thanks for absolutely everything and for being exemplary parents. Mark, Lisa, May, and Grace Fordham for bringing so much love and laughter to the table.

Martin Cross has been a terrific dad to Max and Mia and I thank my lucky stars every day that he met Kay who has been the perfect stepmother and that they have their own fantastic son, Elliott. Martin's Mum, Elsa, has always been an invaluable support.

Mary Herczog, thanks for reading the manuscript of *Plus One* and liking it enough to introduce me to her fabulous literary agent, Christopher Schelling, at Ralph M. Vicinanza Ltd. Thank you Christopher for waving my flag so valiantly and for finding the wonderful John Scognamiglio at Kensington Publishing Corp.

My dear friends Diane Aldred, Gavin Aldred, C.J. and Mike Bigelow, Joel Brand and Kristina Deutsch, Simon Climie, Denise and Nick Gatfield, Lori Leve and Joan Scheibel, Judith Owen and Harry Shearer, Tracey Ullman and Allan McKeown, Marilyn and John Wells have all been incredibly generous to my family and me. I will never forget your kindness.

Tina Jenkins came up with the title among other splendid suggestions. Randi Barnes, Jacqueline Liebman, Peter Morris, Helga Schier, and Tracey Stern also read early drafts and were really helpful and encouraging. Thank you so much.

This has been an incredible journey for me which would not have had such a happy ending (i.e., my book actually getting published) if all of the above and the following people hadn't helped me in some way or believed in me: Gavin de Becker, Jo Burgin, Augusten Burroughs, Robin Danar, Rich Dickerson, Nancy Ditoro, Suzanne Donovan, Mary Alice Drumm, Keri Edwards, Carrie Frazier, Lance Gentile, Simon Gluckman, Melanie Greene, Lisa Grainger Dan Hilderbrand, Steve Hockman, Andrew Kazamia, Joanna Kerns, Haven Kimmel, Suzanne Krull, Geoff Lands, John Lee, Rob Long, Francis Lumen, Amy Mayer, Bob McGowan, Tim Neilson, Lisa Palac, Amy Rappaport, Andrew Rice, Diane Robin, Randi Singer, Moira Steiner, Flody Suarez, Sue Turton, John Watkin, and last but not least, Muttley.

CONTENTS

PLUS ONE

1

End of Part One

As I sipped my glass of Harvey's Bristol Cream, a compulsory tradition on Christmas morning at my parents' home in Hampshire, I watched the torrential rain crash against the kitchen window and imagined I was lying on a sun-kissed Caribbean beach with George Clooney.

I was jolted out of my delicious fantasy when my mother said to me as she surrounded the turkey with soggy brussels sprouts: "I'm worried that you are slipping into middle age without having achieved your potential." It had taken less time than I'd expected to wish I'd stayed in London for the yuletide festivities.

I heard my kid sister, Julia, take a sharp intake of breath as she stifled a gasp. While I pondered my response, I looked back through the window and watched my twenty-year-old son and eighteen-year-old daughter who were supposed to be helping their grandfather carry garden chairs in from the garage but were otherwise engaged in rolling their own cigarettes. I shook my head in disappointment as they lit the cancer sticks and blew smoke rings, while they pretended to be interested in the detailed account of their grandpa's recent game of golf.

It really upsets me that they smoke. But they claim that as they are now adults they can smoke if they want to and hinted that they wouldn't come to Mum and Dad's for Christmas if they weren't granted grown-up status.

"Only in the garden," I'd compromised back in London.

"Deal," they said, and we shook on it.

"I am not middle-aged! I am only forty-one. And I'm not exactly a failure. I have raised two pretty amazing children. They are not heroin addicts or serving time in one of Her Majesty's prisons, which is quite an achievement these days. My daughter is training to be a hair and makeup artist. My son has set up an independent record label and I am a journalist working for one of the biggest and most respected television news organizations in the world, even though they don't pay much," I finally said to Mum, trying very hard not to sound devastated.

Mum waved the smoke away from the roasting tin that she'd just pulled from the oven. "You only work night shifts. It's no wonder you haven't got a boyfriend."

Julia, who is only thirty-three and hasn't got a boyfriend either, refolded the napkins and tried to look invisible. I said: "Mother. Just because my marriage ended in divorce doesn't mean it was a failure. I was only nineteen when I got married." I ignored Mum's "I told you nineteen was too young" look. Mothers can say so much with the twitch of a nose, the raising of an eyebrow, or the purse of a lip.

"Mia is settled in college and now that Max is moving into his own place I shall be open to all offers from suitable gentleman callers."

"I don't know why you got divorced in the first place," Mum mumbled as we carried the turkey with all the trimmings through to the dining room.

My brother, Mark, his wife, Lisa, and their two angelic, adorable, perfect, young daughters were already seated at the dinner table. They are a cross between the Waltons and the Partridge Family—almost too good to be true. Dad struggled to open a bottle of wine with the fancy new corkscrew I'd bought him for Christmas. Things weren't going too well for Dad this Christmas. He'd already set fire to the sleeve of his new shirt as he leant over a candle to pick up the wine bottle. He put his arm in the water jug and the flames were soon out.

My two were fighting over a Christmas cracker. Mia said to Max as they wrestled over the paper hat: "You're so gay."

Max said: "Fuck off."

Luckily Dad didn't hear the gay reference as he takes a very tough line on masculinity. He thinks that men who wear wedding rings or cologne are "poofs." Mum didn't hear the "F" word either or there'd have been trouble. She doesn't believe that anyone who shares her DNA would ever say fuck, let alone do the dreaded deed outside of marriage.

In a bid to change the subject, Lisa said I looked pale. "Is it your period?" she asked sympathetically as she helped herself to gravy.

Mark guffawed. "Women her age don't still have periods."

"At least I've still got all my hair and I don't have a beer belly," I retorted.

He said: "Yes, that's true. You've got a beer bum. You know you really should lose a few pounds if you want to get a boyfriend. And your roots need doing."

Dad pointed the carving knife at Mark and me. "Play nicely or there'll be no television."

The rest of the meal went without a hitch. Julia told us about the latest songs she's written and of her hopes for a new record deal. She lives in Santa Monica, California. She's the youngest in the family and by far the nicest and most successful. Mark is in between.

While Mum was in the kitchen setting fire to the Christmas pudding, Dad tapped his glass with a spoon to gain our attention. He announced: "Tomorrow night your mother will be performing in the chorus of the Hayling Island Operatic Society's production of *Oklahoma!* I expect you all to attend. No excuses and no giggling during the performance. It'll mean a great deal to your mother if all her family is in the audience."

The next night, as we took our seats in the village hall, Dad and Julia sat between Mark and me to separate us, because we are the ones most likely to embarrass the family and bring shame to our door. As the orchestra began the overture, I knew we were in for a rough ride. The curtain opened to reveal a large cast of enthusiastic amateur thespians.

I knew it would be all over if I glanced at Mark so I fixed my gaze on Mum's gingham dress, which she made herself. She used to sew into the early hours to make the many outfits that Julia had to wear for her tap and ballet concerts. Mum didn't have a sewing machine then. Thank God Mia never wanted dancing lessons. Perhaps if she'd dreamed of being a ballerina instead of a hairdresser, she wouldn't sport such exotic hairstyles. Still, this year's mint humbug stripes are an improvement on last year's shocking pink.

It was Dad who cracked up first. His shoulders were shaking up and down uncontrollably. I started laughing despite not having a clue what had caused such mirth. He eventually managed to point out that the male lead singing "the corn is as high as an elephant's eye" at the top of his voice was casting a giant shadow on the wall at the back of the stage. The end of his belt, which was swaying around as he gesticulated, looked like a three-foot penis. Dad and I couldn't take our eyes off the man's shadow and its enormous knob.

I finally managed to explain to my appalled sister what was making Dad and me laugh so much. Soon she too lost it; and then, one by one each family member was let in on the secret until we were all biting our knuckles in a desperate bid to stop howling. No one else in the audience seemed to notice the hysterical shadow, or perhaps they did and just didn't think it was funny.

Mum was not amused. "I've never been so embarrassed in all my life," she said back at the house after the show. "I can't possibly go to next week's audition for the chorus of *The Sound of Music* after this." We all hung our heads in shame and guilt. Then Mum made a dramatic exit to the kitchen to make tea and sandwiches.

When everyone else had gone to bed, Julia and I squeezed another cup of tea out of the pot and pondered the meaning of life.

"Now that both kids have left home, I wonder what the rest of my time on planet earth is going to be like? If I am middle-aged, which I'm not, I don't want Part Two of my life to pass me by without getting some juice out of it. I want adventure and excitement. I want to try something new."

Julia nodded. "You want to be like the mountaineer who died on Mount Everest. She said she'd rather live one year as a lion than a lifetime as a sheep."

I thought about this for a moment. "I wouldn't go that far," I said. "I was thinking more of a change of scenery, not an exhausting and dangerous battle with the elements; besides, I hate the cold. I wouldn't mind a bit of pampering, and I'm sick of being broke all the time."

Then Julia had what was to become my epiphany: "Oh my God! Why don't you come and live with me in California for a year? It's lovely and warm there. You could finally write your book, and you'll stand a much better chance of meeting George Clooney."

"Are you serious?"

"Never been more serious in my life."

Max and Mia thought it was a fantastic idea.

"You go girl," said Mia.

"If anything happens to me while you are gone, please tell my real mother that I love her," said Max.

"Very funny, you little sod. This is serious," I said.

Then Mum walked in and smacked me on the bottom. "Watch your language," she scolded.

"Mum, I'm forty-one not four!" I screeched. Max and Mia howled with laughter.

"I think you should go with Julia," said Mum. "It's time you started thinking about yourself for a change. Before you know it you'll be sixty and these opportunities will stop coming your way."

"Don't let me stop you," Dad said to Mum from behind his newspaper.

Dad also said that I should go but he didn't sound convinced and spent the rest of the evening looking uncharacteristically sad.

That night I dreamed of George Clooney. How could any woman resist him after he saved that boy from the flooded tunnel on *ER*? Later, I saw George interviewed on television and he was so handsome and smart, and handsome and funny, and handsome and stimulating, and handsome and dynamic, and handsome. I was smitten and wished all men looked like him.

Then he successfully made the giant leap from small screen idol to movie star. Once I saw George's perfect naked body in *Out of Sight,* no other actor stood a chance in my book.

In my dream, George walks toward me wearing a white coat with a stethoscope casually draped around his neck.

I look gorgeous in my figure hugging, freshly laundered white uniform and cap. It's ridiculously short but I don't care. I look up from the tray of instruments I am sensuously toying with.

"I need you in cubicle three right away, Nurse Fordham."

"Anything you say, Dr. Ross."

Even though I was going to California for a year I decided to travel light. I gave myself two weeks to sell or give away most of my worldly goods and booked the next available flight to Los Angeles. Once I had made the decision to go, I was fearless and filled with excitement about my new adventure. Hollywood here I come.

2

Sisters Are Doing It . . .

I am experiencing a few communication problems with Americans. No one seems to understand anything I say, yet I speak the Queen's English clearly and succinctly. I ask for a cappuccino and I get a cup of tea, made with lukewarm water. Whenever I speak, people say: "Excuse me?" And I'd have a much nicer day if every American I meet didn't ask me if I am Australian.

Despite the language barrier, I love my new life. I live on the prettiest street in Santa Monica, in the cutest little house, right by the beach, and someone else is paying the rent. Julia is in the enviable and unusual position of being a musician who earns a good living but can still go to the supermarket without being recognized. Not that she goes to the supermarket anymore, as I do all the shopping. It's the least I can do.

If we're not going out, I cook. Thursday night is our favorite night to stay home as it's a good telly night: *Friends*, *Will & Grace*, and *ER*. Life is grand. So long as I can see my kids every three months, everything's going to be just fine. Perfect even.

Now the last thing you do if you live in California is

admit to anyone that you are forty-one, because here, I've discovered, age is all important. Thirty-five, my new Californian friends tell me, is more acceptable, but not much. New mantra: Forty is the new thirty. Forty is the new thirty.

I'm having three months off, then I will get into work mode. Our neighbor, Suzanne, who claims to be twenty-nine, told me: "Most writers here (and who isn't a writer in LA, honey?) head for Starbucks or Peet's with their laptops for a coffee midmorning and make it last all day. Then they stare at their computer screens until their foreheads bleed, hoping for inspiration."

"I've always found the fear of poverty inspiration enough," I said. She then looked around to make sure no one was in earshot and confided, "Coffee shops are great pick-up opportunities but be sure and avoid the advances of the really good-looking men. They are usually in SA."

"What's that?"

"Sex Addicts Anonymous."

Has Julia told everyone in California that I'm looking for a boyfriend?

"Listen honey, there are no secrets on Baxter Avenue," warned Suzanne.

That's true. I've only lived here a few weeks and already I know that Suzanne is an actress who hasn't worked since a six-week recurring guest role on *Nash Bridges,* and has never fully recovered from the disappointment of losing the part of Rachel in *Friends* to Jennifer Aniston. Bitter? You bet.

When I left England for my Californian sabbatical in search of my destiny, I vowed to stop buying so many "things" in Part Two of my life. I brought my Delia Smith cookery book collection with me and the few possessions that I consider precious: my photograph albums; the leather Gladstone bag that my friends in Dorset clubbed together to buy me when I left for London; the box of cards and letters that my children have given me over the years; their baby teeth; and the handwritten Christmas cake recipe my mother gave me more than twenty years ago.

I really ought to know it by heart after all these years. Actually, I do know it by heart already but getting it out and ticking off the list of ingredients is all part of the ritual. It is the thing that defines and connects us. Mum has no idea how much it means to me. Mia can barely rustle up a sandwich so I doubt she'll give a tinker's cuss about the family Christmas cake recipe that's been handed down over generations.

The food here is excellent although the portions are absurdly large. People are either fat or thin in California; there's no in between. Bisexuality seems to be quite fashionable. Some women are so bored waiting for a suitable bloke that they have a relationship with another bird! How thoroughly modern is that? Suzanne told me over lunch at the Broadway Deli on Third Street Promenade about a recent night of passion she'd enjoyed with another woman.

I said: "I didn't realize you are a lesbian."

She said sadly: "I'm not. I'm just lonely."

I said: "I may not have had a date for what seems like an eternity but I'm not ready to start putting from the rough."* I pushed my Chinese chicken salad around the plate for awhile and added wistfully: "Now that I no longer come as a package that includes two children, I might stand more of a chance of meeting Mr. Right instead of Mr. Right Now."

She said: "Stand in line! What makes you think you have more of a chance of meeting a great guy here in California?"

"What sort of a man are you looking for then?" I asked.

"Listen honey, it's tough finding any guy. My last boyfriend

---

* Difficult golfing shot sometimes used to describe lesbian sex.

was fat, broke and unemployed, and he dumped me! If the next man I meet is continent, can chop up his own food and doesn't dribble, I'll have dinner with him. If he hasn't got a crazy ex wife and kids to support he can move in."

I nodded sympathetically and wished she'd stop calling me honey.

Due to some cruel cosmic whimsy I didn't get a chance to meet Sir Paul McCartney at the House of Blues on Sunset Boulevard. He was there to launch his album *Run Devil Run*. I was there because Julia's manager knows someone at his label, Capitol Records, so I tagged along as her "Plus One." As I already mentioned, Julia's a singer-songwriter. Six albums and more than two million copies sold. She's looking for a new record deal but still has a publishing deal that pays the rent and will keep us in tea and cake for another year. Most importantly, Julia still gets invited to lots of events that include a "Plus One."

Anyroadup,* Sir Paul didn't sing at the House of Blues, which was a tad disappointing but at least I managed to see a Beatle in the flesh and we must never forget that there are only two left. Call me shallow but I'm rather enjoying rubbing shoulders with the rich and famous, although my Plus One status closes more doors than it opens. Plus Ones are tolerated rather than welcomed with open arms.

If you are lucky enough to be invited to an event in Hollywood—whether it's a party, a movie premiere, a concert or a store opening—your invitation will usually say Plus One after your name so you won't have to suffer the humiliation of walking in alone or have no one to talk to when you get there. Depending on their status and the event's importance (will *Access Hollywood* be covering it?), a guest might take his

* Northern English for anyway.

or her publicist, manager, agent, boyfriend, girlfriend, sibling, spouse, even a parent if they are recently separated.

If the invitation doesn't say Plus One, then the guest or their representative or the guest pretending to be their own representative if they don't have one will call up to check if they can bring a Plus One. Basically, a Plus One is a guest's guest.

As I was the proud possessor of a VIP pass to The House of Blues to see Sir Paul, I was confident that it would pave the way to an introduction to the great man of song himself. Apart from the fact that I'm a bit partial to a bacon sandwich and don't go soppy at the sight of an animal, we're perfect for each other. Lady Claire McCartney sounds pretty cool too but because my pass, despite being laminated, didn't have a sticker on the back, I couldn't get near him. I bet that model woman Heather he's married had access to all areas.

Brian Wilson (The Beach Boy who wrote the songs, gained five hundred pounds and stayed in bed for ten years) is so famous he didn't need a pass, let alone one with a sticker. He just breezed into Sir Paul's inner sanctum and I got quite huffy with the security guard about it. He wouldn't even discuss the matter, just kept shaking his head. Damn LA and its celebrity guest lists.

As Julia and I waited for the valet* to find our Mustang, she suggested I get over my disappointment about not meeting Sir Paul and concentrate on Sir George. She said, "I read in this week's *People* magazine that George Clooney doesn't want children and you don't want any more. So apart from his preference for women twenty years younger and at least four sizes smaller than you, you're a match made in heaven."

---

* Californians don't like to walk anywhere and will pay anything up to $20 to have a valet park their car for them, even if this means waiting half an hour for them to find your vehicle at the end of the evening.

3

I Want to Be Alone . . .

"Are you sure you'll be okay on your own?" Julia asked me.

"Are you kidding? I can't wait to be alone for two whole weeks. Do you realize I have never really lived on my own? I've never had any space I didn't have to share with a parent, a sister, a husband, or a child. After twenty years bringing up two children, it'll be great to have no one else to cook for or clean up after. I'm so ready for some quality time with me."

I was lying of course. I was petrified. Who in their right mind would ever want to be alone? Julia had arranged a holiday to Fiji long before I moved here and I didn't want her to change plans just because this forty-one-year-old woman didn't know how to keep herself occupied for a fortnight. That would have been too sad and pathetic. I would use the time to reflect on Part One of my life.

I waved Julia off and promptly spring-cleaned the house. That took the best part of a day. Only 312 more hours to fill and I'll have managed to completely avoid thinking about Part One and face the reality that I have no one else to blame for the fact that I have no money, no job, no man and no home to call my own. Things could be worse. I could be forty-one.

I don't remember much of my childhood until Julia was born because her arrival heralded an intrusion on my personal space. We had to share a bedroom until I left home at nineteen to marry Martin, a local builder. It never occurred to me to go to university as no one in my family had ever gone to one.

So when Martin, a handsome man seven years older than me with a job and a car, asked me to marry him I said yes because that was what the women in our family did. We got married and had children. In those days, couples in Weymouth didn't "live in sin" as Mum used to call it and no woman I knew had a career.

We'd only been dating for a couple of months when Martin proposed. Actually, he didn't exactly propose. He asked me to live with him.

"My parents wouldn't let me live with anyone!" I said.

"I'd better marry you then," he said. And he did, three months after my nineteenth birthday. Eighty guests sat down to a three-course meal at the Clarendon Restaurant followed by a disco.

The trouble with not living with someone before you marry is that you don't have the chance to find out if you are compatible. I assumed, wrongly, that once we'd built our own nest, he'd stop going to the pub every night. I also forgot to check if we had the same dreams and aspirations before I promised to stick with Martin 'til death did us part.

In all fairness, neither of us were taught to have dreams and aspirations. Our parents were/are upright, law-abiding citizens, conventional and conformist like most Brits whose childhoods were ravaged by World War II and grew up grateful to still be alive to live simple, uncomplicated lives.

I remember before Max and Mia were born, when I stopped working to be a full-time Mum, standing by the lamppost on Portland Road waiting for a lift to my clerical job at the Ministry of Defense and noting that the same people drove past in the same order every single day to go to their mostly boring, tedious jobs until the day they retired.

I recall thinking at the time that I didn't want a traditional, monotonous life stuck in the same old rut, but I didn't have a spirit of adventure and didn't know how to escape.

I thank my lucky stars every day that Mum and Dad had another daughter who showed me the way.

I could justify leaving Martin when the kids were four and two because he hadn't been the husband I'd hoped he'd be and I didn't want to spend the rest of my life with a man who would rather be at the pub than stay at home with me so I swapped one set of problems for lots of others. Of course, Mum and Dad were devastated and very concerned about what the neighbors would say.

I have a marvelous gift for deleting unhappy thoughts from my memory bank but I seem to recall there followed a long period of chaos, misery, stress, and a distinct lack of cash.

Two years later, I was calling at the former matrimonial home to collect Max and Mia, who had spent the weekend with their Dad, when I began chatting to the lady who lived opposite—the very lady whom Mum and Dad had been sure would have the most to say about the break up. She hadn't realized I'd left at all and, more to the point, couldn't have cared less as she had enough problems of her own.

I thought about what I wanted to do once both kids started school and decided I would like to be a journalist as I'd always enjoyed writing so I began submitting freelance articles to the free weekly, *Dorset Mail*. I'd written to the editor offering my services and signed my name in green ink to make my letter stand out. The editor's horoscope that day had said that the letter "C" and the color green would be significant, so I got the job. Three days a week and I could leave in time to pick up the kids from school. I forgot them once while engrossed in writing a story about the rise in the number of complaints to Weymouth and Portland Borough Council about dog excrement, which British dog owners are none too fussy about cleaning up. It was a subject very dear to my heart. I once wrote a letter to the local evening paper complaining about it myself. I stopped my letter writing campaign when angry dog owners began sending me their dog's turds through the post.

Once I'd spent three months working on the *Dorset Mail*, I felt ready to progress to the *Dorset Evening Echo*. I was excited because this was a newspaper people actually paid to read. I wrote: "CROSSTALK: the weekly page for women that's read by men!" And, as a freelance contributor, I would be able to work from home thus making sure I would never forget to collect the kids from school again!

Martin soon met a terrific girl who loved him for his many qualities. They're still together, go to the pub together, and have a wonderful son of their own who Max and Mia adore.

Martin's mother was always an invaluable support with the kids but didn't like my modern methods of child rearing when they were first born. She was convinced babies should be swaddled and called BBC Radio Solent's Doctor to ask which of us was right. Since she was live on air, there was also a long list of other issues regarding my mothering skills she wanted clarification on and kindly recorded the program just in case I'd missed it. They only mentioned my name and address about six times during the phone-in.

The Radio Doctor explained that there was no right or wrong way, which Mother-In-Law took as a victory for her and continued swaddling my babies when in her care. I decided it wasn't worth falling out over and, for perhaps the only time in my life, didn't argue.

The divorce hit both sets of parents hard. I was definitely the villain of the piece in their eyes as there was another man in the picture and I was the one who broke up the family but that seems a lifetime away now and we all get on well.

I had a few gentleman callers over the years, several actually, including two pathological liars, but no drug addicts or abusers so I consider myself relatively unscathed emotionally by the men I have known. I eventually met a fantastic man who Mum and Dad awarded the "Best So Far" trophy. Steven moved in and we planned a future together, but we never managed to create the happy family life we both wanted. It's very hard to bond with someone else's children when they don't want to bond with you.

Steve's favorite sport was speedway. He went to Poole Stadium every Tuesday night to watch the motorbikes race around a dirt track and eagerly offered to take Max with him to share the fun. Steve was bitterly disappointed that Max thought his beloved sport was "boring."

Another time Steve took us on a "family" day out to a steam engine rally. "Boring," they said. They may have had a point.

When Mia went away to Brownie Camp, Steve decorated her bedroom for her as a surprise and we replaced her single bed with a double—something she'd always wanted. We thought doing this would make her happy and distract her from the fact that Steve had moved his stuff in to the house while she was gone. Max and Mia both adored Steve and were very nice to him, until he moved in.

Mia sobbed for a week and mourned the loss of her old bed for about six months. This was also the time that Max and Mia started arguing about anything and everything. We can't have been easy to live with and, after two years, Steve announced he was leaving. By this time Julia was enjoying considerable success as a singer-songwriter but dropped everything to come and stay with me and took me out for retail therapy.

"The first thing you have to do when you break up with a guy," she said, "is buy a new set of bed linen and throw the old stuff he slept in out." This is very sound advice and must be immediately followed by a new hairstyle, outfit and accessories.

It only took me eighteen months to get over the break up with Steve, and Mia made it clear to any potential stepfathers that they weren't welcome.

After the *Dorset Evening Echo,* television news beckoned and there were freelance gigs for *SKY News*, *BBC South* and *BBC South West* and a weekly anecdotal column for the *Sun*. When the children were fourteen and sixteen we moved to London, with their Dad's agreement, to live in Julia's London home and I began doing shifts at ITN.* Julia was spending most of her time in LA by then.

Mia didn't like living in London but Max and I thrived there. We went to museums, art exhibitions, the theatre occasionally when funds allowed. We tried different restaurants and Max was happy to be part of the conversation when friends came to dinner. Max liked going on trips, doing activities, and playing games like Scrabble and Monopoly. Mia refused to join in most events. She'd fold her arms defiantly and say: "I don't do activities," although she quite liked playing Monopoly on occasion. She thought it pretentious that we lived in a fancy house with a swimming pool. While Max and I couldn't believe our luck and embraced the opportunity, Mia

---

* NBC News.

longed for the time she could either move back to Weymouth or get a council flat.★ Mia lasted three rebellious years in London until she was seventeen and then moved back to Weymouth to live with her dad. We got on much better once we stopped living together.

Max had been talking about getting his own place since he was four. He wanted to be able to drink Coca Cola and watch two videos in a row if he wanted. He finally moved out at the age of twenty, a few weeks before I moved here.

I speak to the kids most days since I arrived in California. We're going to see each other every three months and if they are sick I will catch the next plane home. They insist they are completely cool about my moving to LA to live with their aunt as now they have an exciting place to visit and they won't have to worry about me being lonely.

Of course I'll miss them, but I am very excited about my new life with Julia. Despite the age gap, we've always got on great. When she was young she used to idolize me and was heartbroken when I married and left home. We shared a bedroom when we lived with Mum and Dad. She used to beg me to let her come into my bed for a cuddle. Sometimes if it was really cold, I'd let her come in long enough to warm up my bed and then kick her out for fidgeting. Boy she used to fidget. Still does.

I remember sitting with Mum and Dad and my brother, Mark, at the Café de Paris in London when Julia showcased her first album and how we all finally realized that she has a rare and special gift. Thank God she didn't take Mum and Dad's advice and take a clerical job at IBM but followed her dream to be a singer-songwriter.

I am the first person Julia calls with good news and bad.

★ An apartment in the projects.

Sometimes we talk on the phone five times a day when we are apart. We laugh at the same jokes and finish each other's sentences. Julia has reluctantly agreed to switch off the life-support machine if I am in an irreversible coma. She has also promised to pluck out any witchy hairs on my chin if I am unconscious in a hospital bed and unable to do it myself.

So here I am living in California with my beloved sister. My kids are happy and healthy and for the next year I only have to think about myself for a change. Fantastic. I am officially ready for Part Two. Bring it on.

4

Animal Magic?

As I waited for Julia at LAX Airport, I foolishly allowed myself to get excited about her return. She ran up to me in the arrivals lounge, so elated she could barely speak. "The most amazing thing happened in Fiji," she spluttered. "I found this little puppy dying of starvation on the beach and I've brought it home. Now we've got a dog, we're a proper family. Isn't it wonderful?"

"But you know I don't like dogs. How could you?" I gasped. She muttered some twaddle about a miracle and destiny and we went off to customs to collect "Muttley Puppington." She got all the paperwork sorted and as there's no rabies in Fiji the dog just breezed in. I said: "I don't believe it. You can't get an orange into America but a flea-ridden dog gets carried through like an Arabian prince."

He looked more like a rat than a puppy. Not a hair on his body, all skin and bones. My stomach turned at the thought of this creature peeing and pooing all over our lovely home. Julia promised that the incontinence phase wouldn't last forever. "And anyway," she said. "He only weighs four pounds. He won't grow much bigger. This tiny scrap of gorgeousness won't be any trouble, you'll see." I made it quite clear that I would not be cleaning up any of its "doggy do."

I called Mum and Dad and informed them that their youngest daughter had gone mad. They agreed but said there was nothing they could do, especially as she pays the rent.

We arrived back home with Muttley Puppington to a hero's welcome from the neighbors. They've all got dogs and I must admit that, as dogs go, they are great characters. But if I had a pound for every time one of my children trod in dog muck when they were growing up I'd have been able to buy my own Californian des res.* Cleaning dog shit off football boots was not my favorite pastime.

So, there we were, the neighbors fussing and fawning over Muttley (Julia agreed to drop the Puppington). "Isn't he cute?" (Skinny and bald, remember?) Suzanne cooed as she scratched her own dog, a pit bull called Mary, under its chin: "No wonder you brought that precious bundle of joy all the way from Fiji." Julia beamed proudly like a mother bringing her baby home from the hospital for the first time.

I said bravely while staring at Mary The Pit Bull: "Actually, I'm not much of a dog lover." Total silence and deep shock all round. You'd think I'd just run over one.

Moira from three doors down, an amateur astrologer among other things, took a long inhale of her American Spirit "healthier" cigarette and eyed me suspiciously. "Pisces right?" Then she nodded in a knowing way as if I was the scum of the earth. Moira's dog is a golden retriever called Henry Kissinger.

Then the little bastard, Muttley, tried to bite my foot off. Julia said I was pathetic for screaming so loudly and that he was only playing. She suggested we go to therapy to try to

---

* British term for a desirable residence.

find out why I have such an aversion to dogs. She wasn't joking. Not to put too fine a point on it, I think this bloody dog is going to completely ruin my perfect new life.

Muttley is getting the best veterinary care that money can buy from the Wilshire Animal Hospital and the best chew toys at ten bucks a throw, which he immediately buries in the garden and are never seen again but that doesn't matter because he prefers my shoes anyway.

Julia didn't understand my fury when Muttley first ate one of my shoes.

"It's not like they were Manolo Blahniks," she mocked.

"He's lucky they were my bargain brown sandals from Shoe Pavilion and not my new black loafers from Nine West or I'd have drop kicked the little sod into next door's garden."

Muttley couldn't care less whether the shoes are from Payless, Prada or Jimmy Choo's so long as they are mine. Having brought up two children on a limited budget it's very hard for me to spend more than forty dollars on a pair of shoes. But if I ever do and that little runt eats or buries them, he'll be begging me for a one-way ticket back to Fiji.

Muttley's manicure and pedicure cost twice as much as mine. I've found a marvelous team of Vietnamese ladies on Lincoln who do fingers and toes for $18 ($3 extra for the French manicure). They are a delightful group of women who work seven days a week, never complain and are always smiling. It's a conveyor-belt system that works quite well. "Choose your color," they shout as the next client walks in. Then they carry on chattering among themselves in their incomprehendible language. They tell each customer who asks that the wait is only five minutes but it's usually at least half an hour. The dog's hair and nail care costs $30 at "Doggy Style" but that does include a wash and blow dry.

Muttley sleeps in the most luxurious dog basket you've

ever seen. Green velvet. Not that he spends much time in it. He sleeps most of the night on Julia's lovely, comfy bed.

I, by the way, am sleeping on a lumpy sofa bed in the office area. I call it the office area but it's more accurately described as Muttley's toilet space, the place he prefers to do *his* business.

I actually heard Julia proudly telling Moira that he's so smart, he's already house-trained. Astounding. Just because he did one pee and two poos in the garden she thinks he's house-trained. What about the five "accidents" this week in my bloody room? I've seen the same syndrome in mothers who boast that their toddler is potty-trained just because they managed one pee in the potty. They forget to mention that the poor kid has been forced to sit on it for two hours and any result is more luck than judgment.

Despite the dog's presence, California suits me very well. I've lost six pounds (the fat police are everywhere) and I've finally cracked the art of driving on the wrong side of the road.

Highlight of the week was going to Carrie Fisher's daughter's seventh birthday party in Malibu. Valet parking naturally. I hadn't actually been invited but went with our chum, Judith, who had. Judith is Julia's best friend in LA. She's another British singer-songwriter (Welsh Capricorn) but she acts and does comedy as well. Her dog, Victor, is a longhaired Labrador/husky mix, which Julia used to call the world's most handsome dog until she adopted Muttley.

Judith married a rich and successful American (Is there any other kind?) and knows everyone who's anyone in Hollywood. I might as well officially change my name to Plus One. Judith and I were met at the front door of an unpretentious beach house by the one and only Debbie Reynolds. She smiled warmly: "Hello. I'm Grandma." I wanted to throw myself at her feet and kiss them but said weakly: "Hello Grandma" instead. As *Singin' in the Rain* is one of my all time favorite films, to have one of its stars bring me fried chicken and then clear my plate away was a precious if not a surreal moment. For an all too brief minute, I really felt like somebody.

5

Short Shrift

Muttley is the most spoiled dog in the history of the world. I know I'm not an expert but even I understand that he has to learn who is top dog. Julia has conceded that Muttley appears to be ruling the pack and has to assert himself as the alpha dog.

Just to give you some idea of what I'm up against, Julia goes all soppy and thinks it's sweet when the dog runs off with one of my best shoes or handbag. "Bless him, he's teething."

No reprimand, just proud smiles. But at least he's starting to look like a dog. His fur's grown back and the fleas, worms and ear mites are gone following the liberal use of wildly expensive lotions and potions. He looks like Eddie from *Frasier.* A sort of Jack Russell terrier cross mutant. The vet calls him the world's biggest Jack Russell.

He knows I don't like him. I think he poops in my room on purpose. Even Julia had to admit that his last movement in my room was thoroughly toxic. I told her: "Waving a smoking sage wand in a humorous fashion isn't enough to make me forgive him or you."

Now it smells as if I'm sleeping in a room full of Paxo's

Sage and Onion stuffing.★ The dog's just lying there licking his testicles. He does that most of the day. "Make the most of it, good buddy, because they're not going to be around for long."

At least the people in California are nice. Everyone's so chirpy. I think it's the sunshine that keeps them so up, although it could be the cocaine and the therapy. I think I might set myself up as a therapist. "There is no blame. Now stop whining and move on. That'll be $150. Next!" Easy money.

I might have to break my daily Starbucks habit. Each wet 2 percent grande decaf cup costs $3.45. That's well over a thousand bucks a year and I'm on a tight budget. Plus tip! I said to Julia: "Jesus. Even the cashier who takes your order in a coffee shop expects you to stuff some notes into their tip jar."

Julia said as she sipped her Chai Latte: "Stop worrying about money as Muttley is going to bring us nothing but good luck and fortune."

"Forgive me," I said, "but I can't seem to view that steaming turd he laid in my room this morning as a lucky charm."

Julia is really upset because I don't like her dog. "Everyone else who's met him has fallen in love with him, why can't you?" she pleaded.

He's not crapping in their bedroom is he?

Now that he's had his shots he's allowed to play with the other dogs in the street. He is fearless. His best friends are Henry Kissinger, Victor, and Mary The Pit Bull. (A pit bull—the Great White of the canine family.) I told Julia: "Give Mary a very wide berth. She could have your leg off in a

---

★ Synthetic British stuffing that gets rammed up a turkey's bum post-execution.

heartbeat. They didn't ban pit bulls back home for nothing you know."

I was forced to reconsider my attitude to dogs this week when a dinner guest was making a fuss over Muttley while he licked her face (having previously been licking his bottom, I might add!). She explained how her face was torn apart by a neighbor's dog when she was six. "The plastic surgeon stopped counting the stitches after seventy-five," she said. He did a very good job as she has no scars.

Most incredibly, she isn't scared of dogs and begged the neighbor not to have their dog put down. Yet I run away screaming when Muttley tries to nip at my ankles, so Julia has decided to bring in a trainer.

I grabbed a boogie board in disgust and stormed out of the house to catch some waves. "What do you mean the trainer's for me and not the fucking animal?" If it wasn't for that wretched dog, my life in California would be ideal. I spotted John Boy from *The Waltons* on Third Street. He still looks only about sixteen. I know it's sad but I get a definite adrenaline rush every time I see someone remotely famous.

American stars of stage and screen are so much more thrilling to behold in the flesh than British ones. America has Jennifer Aniston. We have Bet Lynch. America has Brad Pitt and George Clooney. We have Robert Carlyle and Robbie Col-trane. Yes we have Hugh Grant, but he's not Tom Cruise is he? We have Emma Thompson. America has Julia Roberts. This is not an acting competition. I'm talking glamour and star quality.

Although fellow Brit sisters Joan and Jackie Collins are glamorous and ooze star quality, Julia and I are more like Lyn and Vanessa Redgrave with a liberal sprinkling of Dawn French and Jennifer Saunders. In some quarters we are mentioned in the same breath as those infamous saucy American siblings: The Hiltons. We're more the Over The Hilltons.

Certainly there's no shame in being British in California. British celebrities are hot right now. Tracey Ullman led the way. Americans love Jennifer Saunders and Ab Fab. They love Sharon Osbourne. They don't love but respect Anne Robinson. And as for Princess Di and Bridget Jones, well, they are obsessed. Sheena Easton still gets a fairly positive nod. It's not just British girls who are popular here. Americans are crazy about Simon Cowell, Tony Blair, and Harry Potter.

The biggest buzz of the week for me was to gaze upon the gorgeousness of David Duchovny at a showbiz party in Beverly Hills (or Heavily Bills as we poor folk call it). He is so tall and handsome that it was very hard not to stare. I call him David Do-Shag-Me. Not to his face obviously. We haven't actually been introduced, but Julia is pally with his manager and her husband who were hosting the gathering. She sang at their wedding, which was a very grand affair apparently. They do give a very good party.

Corbin Bernsen was at this particular bash too. I used to have quite a crush on him when he was in *LA Law*. I laughed far too loudly when he pretended he'd vomited up his plate of trifle. I think we'd both had one too many vodka gimlets.

I was relieved to see that Corbin Bernsen is tall. Stars of stage and screen are often challenged in the height department. Not that I'd kick Tom Cruise or Mel Gibson out of bed for eating crackers. I do hope My George is one of the tall ones.

6

Hubble Bubble . . .

I have introduced Moira and Suzanne to the joy of afternoon tea and every month we meet other friends at a different fabulous hotel for cake and sandwiches. Our favorite is the Beverly Wilshire, but we've heard very good reports about the Peninsula and are planning to try that soon. Thank God everywhere in America takes credit cards.

So here we are drinking Earl Grey out of proper china cups and eating cucumber sandwiches with the ends cut off when a lady I've not met before, who's been invited by Moira's sister, Naomi, suggests she hosts a Pink Witches night in my honor to welcome me to California. Excuse me?

This woman is a Transformational Clairvoyant who "uses her natural intuitive abilities to help you make the changes that you want to make in your personal or business life." I see.

She's also a licensed minister with the Human Energy Church who can marry you or bury you. She tells us to each bring a home-cooked organic dish to eat, an item of special significance to us that we will give to a fellow pink witch during the ceremony, and we are to wear something pink.

As I drive to the Transformational Clairvoyant's house, I say to Julia: "We should think ourselves lucky we aren't virgins or we might end up getting ceremonially shagged." Mind you, in my current state of enforced celibacy, I might be the first to volunteer.

We arrive at an isolated house, in the dark with owls hooting, to be greeted by three gorgeous young men who are valet parking the cars. Things are looking up. The Transformational Clairvoyant/Chief Pink Witch's house is stunning. She's set the most beautiful round table in the courtyard. There are eleven places because, she says, eleven means strength and freedom. A tarot card has been randomly placed at every table setting, the idea being that we will intuitively sit at the right one for us. I long to get the best card just as I had prayed the package would stop with me as a child during pass the parcel.* It never did of course.

Each plate has a perfect pink rose with the thorns removed placed on it. The table is covered in fresh lavender (good for self-esteem, apparently), and there are clear crystals, pink candles, and pink flowers on every surface.

There is the most wonderfully calm atmosphere. Blissful even. My tarot card is the Queen of Cups. She is someone who is willing to go deep into her emotions to get who or what she loves. The cups are emotions and the queen is the inner mastery card. There is something about the eleven card for me as well, which means letting go and lust!

If I had sat just one place to the left, which I'd been seriously considering, I'd have had the Empress; but Naomi sat there. This was actually very apt as Naomi, who is a tall, slim blonde and a gorgeous former model with a peaches-and-

---

* Favorite British children's party game where the gift has been wrapped many times, and each time the music stops the child left holding the gift takes off a layer of wrapping. The winner is the kid who takes off the last layer and he or she gets to keep the gift. The game is usually rigged so that the kid whose birthday it is wins.

cream complexion, has a perfect life—a fabulous home in the Hollywood Hills, no job, and a handsome, wealthy husband who adores her.

Well, her life isn't exactly perfect. She has endured fertility treatments for some years. Did you know that once you get to forty you only have a 5 percent chance of conceiving naturally? Getting older really sucks. Thank God I had my children when I was in my twenties.

We pink witches write a wish on a card. I wish for love and a well-paid job. We go around the table, clockwise, and each of us says something for which we are thankful.

Moira lifts up her sweater and shows us her magnificent 34DDs. "I give thanks every day for my marvelous boobs." We nod in agreement. They are very impressive. Moira knows what every celebrity's star sign is and can remember the star signs of all her friends' boyfriends going back years. If anyone is having a bad day it's because Mercury is in retrograde. If it's a good day it's the dawning of the Age of Aquarius.

Julia gives thanks for Muttley. She notices my hurt and disappointed look and adds: "And my sister."

Julia's priorities may have changed somewhat since she found Muttley, but we are still soul mates. Sometimes I think she is otherworldly because her capacity to love unconditionally and see the best in everyone and every situation is of almost saintly proportions. Her work ethic and ability to cut through the oceans of crap within the music industry stuns and truly inspires me.

She can make an audience weep with the sheer beauty of her remarkable voice. Then she makes them laugh out loud as she explains how her extraordinary songs came to be written. Not only is she generous of spirit, she is generous with her hard earned cash. Family, friends and charity have all benefited from her success and no one more than me.

When I told Julia that I found it demeaning to ask her for housekeeping money every week, she arranged for all her bank accounts and credit cards to be made into joint ones and handed me the cards as if it was the most natural thing in the world.

But despite everything she has done for me, I am still furious with her for bringing the dog into my life without consulting me.

Moira reckons that the reason Julia and I get on so well is because she's a Leo, which is the most easygoing sign, and I'm not in competition with her as a singer. "And," Moira says, "you don't like Muttley because you are jealous of him. You don't like sharing your sister with anyone else. Pisces women are very controlling."

I say: "Interesting."

I think: "Bollocks."

We all toast one another having been instructed by the Transformational Clairvoyant to look one another in the eye as we do so, which is actually very hard to do. The degree of difficulty is up there with looking at yourself in the mirror and saying "I love you."

The Transformational Clairvoyant, a pretty, soft-spoken woman in her mid forties with a curly, light brown Vidal Sassoon bob, then gives us each a pink Madonna candle figure (Madonna—mother of Jesus, not Rocco). We carve our names on the bottom, then decorate it with colored glitter pens. The idea being we make Madonna look how we want to be. I give mine very long hair.

Another pink witch, a complete stranger to me, Aurora, tells us she is being courted by a man she met at an AA meeting and holds high hopes that he might be "the one." This is quite a stretch for her as for the past five years she's only been "involved" with women. She muses: "A hermaphrodite would be perfect for me. They've got the whole kit and caboodle—the toad, the hole *and* the pudding."

Suzanne nods: "You sleep with thirteen or fourteen women and suddenly you're a lesbian!"

Judith is very excited as she has just finished recording her album and a marketing executive at her record company told her: "If this record doesn't sell upward of three million, there's something wrong with this industry." We drink to that.

Christine, who's a doctor, tells us how her mother-in-law kept interrupting her while she was on the telephone trying to organize an emergency airlift for a critically ill patient, to ask why she didn't have any strawberry ice cream.

Moira runs her hand through her long blond hair and tells us about the time her boyfriend of five years came to her house and found her in bed with another man. "How did he react?" we chorus.

"He burst into tears." She sucks heavily on her cigarette and continues, "Well, what do you expect from an Aries with Scorpio rising in a Sagittarius moon." We nod sagely.

On that note, we take our wax Madonnas to an altar that the Transformational Clairvoyant has prepared, place them in a huge pot of sand and light them while at the same time saying our desires out loud, followed by "so be it."

Naomi wishes for a baby. Naomi and her husband are giving fertility treatment one last attempt. Naomi is the sweetest, kindest woman whose capacity to bring sunshine into our lives is only eclipsed by her ability to shop. If ever Julia or I want to buy something we call Naomi and she'll tell us what we need and where to buy it for the best price.

We finally go back inside the Transformational Clairvoyant's house where Naomi shows us fifty Pashmina shawls that one of her other friends, who wasn't invited to Pink Witches Night, sells at cost price. We all buy one at $150 a pop and

club together to buy a red one for the Transformational Clairvoyant as a thank you. Commerce is never far away in California.

Aurora hugs me good-bye and tells me how much she
loves me and wants to meet for lunch. I don't think so.
Californian women are a bit too casual with their hugs and "I
love you's" if you ask me. Julia says I'm repressed.

As we drive home, I tell Julia: "If I don't find a man after
all that hocus-pocus, you can dip me in honey and throw me
to the lesbians."

7

Gone with the Wind

I must admit that the dog trainer was worth every cent of his $120. Muttley can now sit and lie down on command. He's stopped yapping and sits patiently while we eat our dinner without trying to steal food from our plates.

When he starts nipping, we give him a toy to chew. I was taught to pick him up and hold his collar in such a fashion that he can't nip me, but I told the trainer: "That bit of advice won't be necessary as I never touch him."

Now that he's finally responding to commands, I'm beginning to warm to him ever so slightly. And he's doing his "outsides" outside. I don't think I'll ever achieve the same dizzy heights of dotage as Julia, who just marvels at the sight and texture of one of his turds. "And they don't even smell," she gasps proudly. Sweet Jesus!

But we have had a breakthrough. Literally. Earlier this week I was quite worried about him. His stomach had swelled overnight to twice its normal size. I thought he might have cancer and be on his last legs. I know I resent his presence but I don't want him to die.

I put him on my lap and gently stroked his back. He let out the most heinous fart. He deflated before my very eyes, looked at me apologetically and gave an embarrassed chuckle. I think that was the moment we bonded ever so slightly as I knew exactly how he felt.

We later discovered he'd managed to get into his food cupboard and had stuffed himself with dried dog food. Ours is a very smart dog.

Moira was looking after him while we went to a BAFTA (British Academy of Film and Television Arts) Garden Party. It's well worth being a member for the screenings alone, and you can use your membership card to get into the cinema to see nominated films for free in the months leading up to the Oscars. Julia's a member, and I go to all the BAFTA events as her Plus One.

The only famous people I clocked at the bash were Christopher Casenove and Jaqueline Bisset. I met Minnie Driver's sister, Kate, who is absolutely stunning. I didn't ask her what she did for a living, if anything, as I was too busy looking for signs of plastic surgery. It's not natural and it's not fair on the rest of us to look that perfect. I wonder if Minnie and Kate get on as well as Julia and I do? Moira told me later that Kate Driver is a film producer. I should have guessed— most people are in this town.

We declined an invitation from a bunch of Welsh film producers (oxymoron?) to another party, which was just as well as I might have missed the chance to meet the War Correspondent.

Moira was entertaining two handsome men when we went to collect Muttley. She used to go to school with one of them. The men were seasoned hacks who were swapping Kosovo stories when we arrived. These were men who knew their Tutsis* from their Hutus.* There's something intriguing about a man who's been to war. Sigh!

* Warring tribes in Rwanda.

They came back to our house as Moira was tired and wanted an early night. One thing led to another and I ended up sharing my bed settee with the War Correspondent. Well, we had a lot in common. I shall spare you the gory details, dear reader. Suffice to say, it wasn't just the sofa bed that moved.

Julia has a date with the Bureau Chief next week. As she is clearly playing by the proper rules of engagement, I have been christened Slutty Spice while she is Repressed Spice. And she's been banging on and on about how if we didn't have the dog, we wouldn't have had to ask Moira to look after him and I wouldn't have met the War Correspondent when we went to collect him.

Moira, Judith and Suzanne burst into spontaneous applause when I stepped onto the porch the following morning to pick up the *LA Times*. I have been greeted with high fives and shouts of "respect!" from everyone on the street. Nothing is sacred. I haven't mentioned to anyone that this is the first time I've ever done anything so reckless and exciting as I don't want to spoil my new image as a femme fatale.

I have now got my groove back and have officially declared our house a war zone. At least I'll have a good answer when my grandchildren ask: "What did you do in the war, Grannie?"

8

Dangerous Liaisons

Julia insisted on taking a photograph of me the day after my bedroom romp with the War Correspondent as I had such a healthy glow. It would have been churlish not to put it in a frame.

I was brought down to earth with a heavy bump when Christine, the Doctor, who specializes in HIV and AIDS, demanded confirmation that a condom had been worn.

"How can I expect Max and Mia to use condoms if I don't?"

"Did you use a condom?"

"YES!"

Every time a man has unprotected sex with a woman infected with gonorrhea he has a one in three chance of catching it from her, she lectured. "A woman has a 75 percent chance of catching gonorrhea from an infected man if they have unprotected sex because semen lingers," she said without a hint of embarrassment. I felt like a naughty pupil standing before a strict headmaster except that Christine is tall and beautiful with long fair hair. The very hair to which I myself aspire.

My hair is at that horrible in-between stage, neither long

nor short. Shoulder length. Lackluster and lank. Highlights no longer suffice and I need the roots done as well. Julia sports the same Vidal Sassoon bob that has served her very well for some years. Her hair is much thicker than mine and grows a lot faster. She's a couple of inches taller than me as well. The only thing I've got that she hasn't is an overdraft. And cleavage, if we're being honest.

But I digress. Christine told me that if you sleep with a man infected with HIV (not that you'd know), you have a 1 in a 1,000 chance of catching it if you have unprotected vaginal sex—1 in a 100 if you have anal sex.

She said: "Most men lie about their bisexuality or intravenous drug use. I'm treating two heterosexual women who caught HIV from their bisexual husbands, who deny that they have ever slept with a man despite medical evidence to the contrary, and claim they caught it from infected barbers while having a wet shave."

But the good news is that she hasn't lost a patient to AIDS for a year; and in LA, the expensive treatment for HIV and AIDS is paid for by the government if you are uninsured. The side effects from the drugs are debilitating whether your insurer or the government pays.

Terrific. I think Julia was secretly delighted to watch me squirm as I had become unbearably smug since my sound shagging. Still, at least she had her date with the Bureau Chief to look forward to.

I laughed out loud when he called to say that his much younger sister (twenty, second marriage) was in town visiting and that he'd have to bring her on the date as well. Julia handled the news brilliantly. Quick as a flash she suggested that she bring her sister along. A foursome! The Bureau Chief's sister reminded me of Bette Midler on speed. She wanted to go to Santa Monica Pier. So we did.

I took it upon myself to take her on the big wheel and bumper cars so the dating couple could have some quality time alone. But from where I was looking (the top of the big wheel and stuffing my face with candy floss) they seemed to be sitting in silence. I had a great time.

The Bureau Chief was off to cover some skirmish the next day so there was no chance for him to get to know Julia better, certainly not with his manic kid sister attached to his hip. What was he thinking? But I'm confident that any sexual activity that might have occurred between them would have been perfectly safe as Julia is a high-ranking member of the Condom Police. She doesn't accept that it's like eating a banana with the skin on and insists that if it's not on, it's not on.

I have purchased a fabulous new bed with a sexy mosquito net draped over it. "That was the last and only time I'll ever do it on a sofa bed," I told Julia as I carefully arranged the material. "The next time it will be romantic and comfortable. And safe, of course."

New mantra: "I will have sex again before I die."

9

Upon My Sole!

The bloody dog has ripped my mosquito net to shreds. Julia tried to laugh it off: "We don't suffer with mosquitoes anyway. The last thing that bit you was the War Correspondent."

I said: "It wasn't meant to be functional, it was more a prop to lend an air of sexy romance and transform my boring bedroom into a boudoir. The main point being that it was mine and your fucking dog destroyed it."

I was an inch away from packing my bags and catching the next flight out of LA, but as I had nowhere to go I had to back down.

My bedroom is my own little sanctuary for which Muttley has no respect. I'd put down a lovely new rug from IKEA that nicely covered all the dirty patches he'd made on the old one. Okay, so white is not exactly a sensible color; but if he's as smart as Julia says he is, he could learn to wipe his paws before he walks in.

I felt quite sorry for Mutts after four of his teeth fell out. I'd carelessly left an empty plastic bottle lying around that the hound thought would make an excellent chew toy, but it was a bit much for him.

Julia said: "What were you thinking?"

"How was I to know puppies have baby teeth? I suppose they're going to be replaced with even bigger fangs," I said.

Julia graciously cleaned up the mess. She got most of the stains out and has kept the teeth to put under his pillow. But just when I thought he couldn't do anything to hurt me again, he ate my favorite pair of sandals.

If you're very lucky, once in your life you find the perfect pair of shoes. Shoes that never give you blisters or make your feet ache. They are so comfy you don't even know you're wearing them. Muttley ate mine. Well, one of them. Lucky for him they cost less than $40.

He eats anything and everything: candles, pens, magazines, flowers and plants, lampshades, the television remote control; and he took several bites out of Julia's yoga mat! She didn't even flinch when he chewed her Pashmina shawl. Mind you, everyone's got one now and they are officially passé. You can't give them away.

Julia still thinks that we're lucky to have him. She said: "The man in the pet shop said he'd cost $800 to buy."

I said: "He's already cost us three times that in vets bills and furniture snacks and he's only four months old!"

Now she's employing a professional dog sitter to keep him company so he won't get bored and eat our stuff when we go out. Madness. I am somewhat consoled because tomorrow he's having his testicles cut off. "At least there won't be any more Muttleys running around eating peoples' prized possessions," I said.

The vet has also assured us that, once he's been castrated, he will stop emitting so much green semen, which he leaves all over my white bed linen. It is florescent green and truly repugnant. He likes to lie on my bed between the hours of 10 A.M. and 1 P.M. because the sun shines through the window and he prefers a sunny spot. Julia bought me a dark blue blanket to protect the bed, but he always manages to find the square inch that isn't covered.

I suggested to Julia that we should get rid of him before he literally eats us out of house and home and every surface is bright green. "I don't mean flush him down the toilet," I said, "but give him to a good home—a home that's already shabby and whose owners have no social life."

I wrote a list of pros and cons for us to weigh up. I had fifty-six cons and no pros. In the spirit of fairness, I let Julia put the case for the defense. After two hours deliberation, she came up with no cons and two pros: (1) he has a very cute face, and (2) he makes me laugh out loud at least once every day.

Bugger. It's her house so the dog stays. His face isn't even that cute.

10

A Shitty Business

Julia has gone to London to meet with her music publisher, so I have to be responsible for Muttley for two weeks. As I am living in Julia's house rent-free, it's the least I can do. But it's another reminder that financial independence gives you the freedom to choose where and how you live and I feel sadly lacking in the choice department at the moment.

What has happened to me? I moved to LA in search of excitement and here I am in search of excrement.

However, I've always felt strongly that the world would be a much better place if all dog owners cleaned up their doggy's do and, as I've already mentioned, I've had letters published on the subject, so I am going to take my responsibility seriously.

Knowing that in all likelihood I would retch the first time I did it, I felt it wise to have a dress rehearsal. A good technique is vital. The action must be quick and efficient.

I carried out the dummy run in the privacy of our own yard, checking first that no one was looking. A neat pile of stones was carefully arranged for me to scoop up with my plastic bag in one fell swoop. You place your hand inside the bag, grab the poo, pull the bag inside out, tie it in a knot, hold it at arm's length, hold your breath, and place it in the nearest bin. Actually, it's best to hold your breath from the off.

Moira and Suzanne heard my shrieks and rushed to my aid. I had failed to check that the bag didn't have a huge hole in it and picked up the stones in my bare hands. Imagine if it had been the real thing? I swear they'd have had to carry me off in a straitjacket.

Muttley continues to rule the roost. He still can't be trusted in the house alone, so we still engage the services of the neighborhood dog sitter. She takes her job very seriously. One neighbor was sitting in a daily writers' meeting where interruptions were banned. He'd hired the dog sitter for the first time that day. A secretary came in and handed him a note. All eyes were on him as he carefully studied it. They knew it had to be important, perhaps even a death in the family. He nodded and sighed in as concerned a way as he could muster as he read: "Dear Rob, I took Kaheba for her morning walk at 10:30. She did a number one but not a number two."

The first time the Dog Lady dog sat for Muttley she left a note saying he'd done a number two during their evening stroll but not a number one. I asked Julia incredulously: "Whoever heard of anyone, man or beast, doing a number two without a number one?"

Julia lets Muttley sleep on her bed every night, so I had to afford him the same luxury while she was away for fear of giving him abandonment issues. Her fear, not mine. He has every other facility, why not his own psychiatrist?

Muttley was surprisingly easy to sleep with. He didn't fidget or snore and somehow always ended up under the duvet with his head on a pillow. That was weird enough until the morning we woke up in the spoon position. I hate to admit it but I might have to reconsider my feelings toward Muttley. It won't be a complete surrender though. I will keep notes of all his crimes and misdemeanors.

How did Muttley repay me for my kindness while Julia was away? He gave me fleas. I thought I had shingles at first but the doctor said they were fleabites. Julia insists she told me I was supposed to give him a special bath to keep his fleas at bay.

"I definitely told you to give him a flea bath."

"You did not."

"You've just forgotten, Auntie Alzheimers."

"Don't call me Auntie Alzheimers."

I thought Max and Mia made a fuss when I washed their hair when they were toddlers, but I never had to wrestle them to the ground to get a lather. By the end of Muttley's bath time, I was totally exhausted, soaking wet, and covered in suds. It was like having another child except my children never gave me fleas—head lice and verrucas, but not fleas.

11

Anyone for Tennis?

The dog has been a little bastard this week. We stopped using the services of the Dog Lady every time we went out as it was costing a small fortune and Julia was sure that he was no longer a "bad dog." But every time we went out and left him alone, we returned to a war zone. He's started opening the food cupboards. He ate all his treats, two packets of Puffins, and scattered a bag of sugar over the floor. Shredded papers and books were everywhere and drawers were ransacked.

He ate the new Atlas that cost $75 and other really expensive, arty-farty, coffee table books that were just for show. The second night when he ate Julia's prized possession—a personally signed, collector's edition CD by Her Holiness, Joni Mitchell—I thought Julia might have had her fill of the Mutt, but she forgave him after an hour.

He even ate master recordings of some of Julia's new songs. She tried to convince herself that it wasn't him but had to accept the sad, sorry truth when we saw the tape trailing out of his bum.

He ate the new shoes that Julia had bought me to replace the previous ones that he scoffed, and he ate the couch. I am not joking. He ripped the couch apart and scattered the con-

tents all over the floor. The mess and damage were unbeliev-
able. A kind of exhaustion set in, like a brief lull in a long,
long war.

We've got a man coming in at the weekend to fit locks on
all the cupboard doors, and we've brought Muttley a magnificent kennel so we can leave him outside when we go out in
future. I call it Muttley's apartment. Needless to say, he won't
go in it.

I sulked for two days. Julia bought me a new tennis outfit
by way of compensation but it was not enough; I was clini-
cally depressed. I knew exactly what I needed . . .

As Julia had dinner plans that didn't include me, I invited my
handsome, virile, amusing, and very young tennis buddy over
to the house for martinis and dinner. He's an actor I met at
Suzanne's. We've been meeting for a weekly game of tennis. I
decided that life is too short to follow "the rules" and suggested to him that we might sleep together. Quite bold I
know, but I keep reading that it's okay for a woman to make
the first move so long as you don't want him to marry you.
Tennis Man readily agreed.

But Muttley was ready for an offensive. He refused to get
off the bed for a start. Tennis Man valiantly pushed Muttley
off with his foot several times, but we finally had to interrup-
tus the coitus when Muttley became royally stuck under the
bed. It took a Herculean effort to get him out, which was all
the more difficult a maneuver as I was desperately trying to
ensure that Tennis Man, who is ten years younger than me,
didn't get a glimpse of my ample naked bottom.

Then, just when I thought things couldn't get any worse,
Muttley wolfed down the used condom that Tennis Man had
carelessly abandoned on the floor by the bed. I looked at

Muttley solemnly and said: "This time you've bitten off more than you can chew."

The next morning Julia became alarmed that Muttley was trembling and had a rasp in his throat every time he exhaled.

I confessed all about the rubbery snack. Luckily, she saw the funny side. Her telephone conversation with the vet's assistant was priceless. We were told in hushed and deadly serious tones that this was a potentially dangerous situation and that if Muttley hadn't passed the condom within 24 hours, he'd have to have an X-ray and undergo a surgical procedure. I told Julia: "Hopefully they'll extract it anally. That'll teach the little shit to eat everything in sight."

We went out that night and left a note for the Dog Lady just in case Muttley was taken ill or passed the condom (sounds like a good parlor game). As the Dog Lady is such a straighty pants, I suggested we say he'd swallowed a balloon.

Muttley successfully and painlessly passed the condom that night. I said to Julia as she covered him in a blanket: "Lucky for him it was lubricated."

12

Bottoms Up

"I think Mum may be right and I am slipping into middle age," I said to Julia as we strolled barefoot along the beach. "Last week I forgot which floor I parked the car on in the multistory and put the car keys in the fridge. It's no wonder you've started calling me Auntie Alzheimers. Then there was the white eyebrow hair that came back the day after I plucked it out. I've got two gray pubic hairs for Christ's sake!"

Julia nodded unhelpfully: "And you have been taking a lot of afternoon naps lately." She tried to make me feel better: "The older the violin, the sweeter the tune."

I groaned. "If I start peeing my pants just smother me with a pillow. My life is over." I walked home dejected and climbed into bed and hid under the duvet for three hours.

When I resurfaced, Julia suggested I start going to a yoga class with her. "You need to work on your Mind Body Spirit," she said.

"It's too late for yoga. I need liposuction, botox, and a brain transplant." But she insisted.

Now if you're feeling middle-aged, fat, and frumpy, the last thing I'd recommend is a yoga class in California. I whispered to Julia as we assumed the warrior position: "Everyone in this class is thinner and prettier than me. Including the men."

The best thing about the class is the yoga teacher, who is very cute. I'm not convinced that cobras and downward dogs are the answer to all the world's problems but I have found that I am less bothered by Muttley's antics than I used to be. I find all that "Om" chanting acutely embarrassing but manage to say it out loud by pretending that it means "Stick It Up Your Arse."

Julia says my hair's been in much better condition since I started having the occasional sleep over with Tennis Man. Even the Hair Lady noticed my hair was looking good. I suggested she also take a younger lover but she told me that she had made a pledge to God. "I'm saving myself for my future husband," she said.

"Excuse me?" I said. "Say you never meet Mr. Right? You might never know the joy of sex." But there was no budging her. She would remain *virgo intacta* until her wedding night. "It will make my marriage and my husband's commitment and love even stronger. I don't condemn you for what you are doing but sex outside of marriage isn't for me. I've set my boundaries," she said. Snogging★ is okay but not intercourse.

I know what she means about boundaries. Suzanne was discussing anal sex with Moira as we took afternoon tea at the Peninsula Hotel. They clearly hadn't heard Christine the Doctor's terrifying statistics. "I'm sorry," I told them, "he can put his sausage in my honey pot but no man is putting his dangly toilet part up my Queen Mum."†

Which reminds me of the story told to me by a record producer during a most excellent dinner at the Ivy about a

---

★ Passionate kissing.
† Cockney rhyming slang for "bum."

gay guitarist (no names no pack drill★) who went to the doctor because he had a sharp pain in his bottom. He told the
doctor as he was being examined: "It's right there by the en-
trance, doctor."

The doctor replied coldly: "In my profession we call it the
exit."

★I have no idea of its literal meaning (it's just an expression for God's sake!),
but it is commonly used to indicate that one is not prepared to divulge the
name of the person or persons who told you the information. Probably dates
back to World War I when people were warned not to say anything to anyone for fear of giving secrets to the enemy.

13

Naked Ambition

We've come to the Philippines as Julia has been invited to play five gigs here. Much to our amusement and delight, Julia's very big in the Philippines and gets treated like a proper diva. They call her "The Jewel of Pop Jazz." The money she's getting paid will pay the rent and keep us in tea and cake for a whole year.

Julia felt it best that Muttley be looked after by a family member, so my son is looking after her son in LA. Even with the price of his flight and paying his rent in London for a fortnight, Max was cheaper than the Dog Lady.

Julia and I were met at Manila airport with bouquets and garlands and paparazzi, then VIP treatment—straight through immigration and customs with a staff member to collect our luggage. Luxury hotel. Bloody fantastic. I couldn't stop singing: "I love our life. I love our life. I love our life."

The first two gigs were corporate ones where big businesses pay an absurd amount of money to entertain their customers and staff at a tax deductible promotional knees up.★

★ A lively party or gathering taken from the popular British song: "Knees Up Mother Brown."

The trouble with this sort of gig is that the audience is often drunk and doesn't give a flying fig who is singing. They just want to chat loudly at the bar.

The opening act didn't have a hope in hell of getting their attention. Opening acts have the toughest time of all as usually nobody wants to hear them, apart from their friends and family. Julia had to work really hard to win the audience and sensibly ignored my advice to take the money and run.

As we drank tea in our hotel room after the gig Julia told me: "It's very hard being an artist on the road. Not all glamour. People's expectations are so high and they are very critical. You're either too fat or too thin or they prefer Celine Dion. I can't tell you how lonely I was before you came."

I offered to tuck her into bed like I used to when she was a kid. She bolted upright from her snug position under the covers. "Tuck me in like you used to when I was a kid? You never tucked me in. You'd let me into your bed for a cuddle after I begged you, but you only let me stay long enough to warm up your bed for you and then you kicked me out."

I chuckled. "Here we are thirty years later and we're still sharing a bedroom."

Julia said: "But we didn't have room service then."

"Yes we did," I said. "Mum."

Most artists have a special someone who is their right-hand person/companion/flunky on the road. Celine Dion's sister, Manon, travels with her all the time.

For the past thirty years, Julia and I have had pet names for each other that have to begin with B. When on tour Julia is Celine and I am Manon, so we become Beline and Banon. And there the similarity ends. I read in *People* magazine that Celine pays Manon $100,000 a year.

I said to Julia as I carried her bags through the hotel lobby: "I trust when you eventually sign a new record deal, I can officially go on the pay roll." But she didn't hear, she was too busy signing autographs.

One of my functions as Julia's "assister" is to hold her hair dryer while she coifs her locks. I said sadly: "I don't want to be holding your hair dryer when I'm fifty."

Julia said: "Get a job then. Or marry a millionaire."

Interesting. The women I know who have wealthy husbands do seem very happy and content. Some of them actually love their spouses. Financial independence is obviously preferable but would it be such a terrible thing to have a rich husband?

Later, while Julia and I were swimming in the hotel pool, she turned to me and whispered: "I know exactly how Geri Haliwell* must have felt. It's horrible having people stare at you while you try to swim."

Geri stayed at our hotel some months before but wasn't a popular guest because, we were told by a wonderfully indiscreet waiter, she screamed at staff and fellow guests to stop staring at her while she swam in the hotel pool.

I said: "Julia, people are staring because the plastic swimming hat you insist on wearing to protect your hair from the chlorine is so tight it pushes your forehead into the deepest frown and makes you look like a Klingon."†

The next day as I washed my smalls‡ in the sink, I thought about how hard it must be for superstars to lead normal lives. Madonna's manicurist used to sell her nail cuttings to fans. So I wasn't too surprised when Julia said: "Don't use the laundry service in case the staff hold up our dirty underwear for all their colleagues to see."

As I don't like hand washing clothes or pots unless I'm

---

* The artist formerly known as Ginger Spice.
† Legendary bad guys in *Star Trek*.
‡ Small items of clothing like bras and knickers.

wearing my Marigolds★ (bad for the hands darlings), which I hadn't packed, I decided to improvise.

The best I could come up with were the plastic bags the complimentary newspapers came in. I'd just got out of the bath so I was naked. The plastic bags didn't match but I wore them anyway.

Doorbell goes mid-scrub and I assumed it was Julia. Wrong. Boy did we keep those porters entertained. I was mortified.

It was not a good start to my birthday. The most pleasing thing anyone can say to me is: "We're upgrading you to first class." A close second is: "Are you or your sister the oldest?"

Feeling like I'd passed my sell by date, I told Julia: "I don't want you to tell any of our Filipino friends that it's my birthday. I don't want any fuss." What I really meant was that I didn't want to have to tell anyone that I was forty-two.

As we walked into the rehearsal studio, a thirty-piece orchestra, the band, and five singers burst into "Happy Birthday." I was presented with flowers, chocolates, and a basket of tropical fruits that was so heavy it needed three grown men to carry it. I was very glad that Julia had disobeyed me.

Much to my surprise, when we finally made it back to the hotel after the usual crawl through Manila's unbearable traffic, Julia suggested we go to the bar for a birthday drink. We'd been in bed by 8 P.M. every night since we arrived. Julia is not a party animal and doesn't drink, which can be a bit of a drag. She is so allergic to alcohol that she gets drunk after one sip, so I ordered champagne for me and a ginger ale for her. Then we eyed the many handsome men who surrounded us.

No one approached us for a chat or a flirt, either out of

★ Leading brand of rubber gloves.

deference to Julia's Divaness or the usual assumption that we were lesbians. One man finally approached us. "Hello," I said, "we're sisters, not lesbians." Julia looked at me disapprovingly. "How else will they know for God's sake?" I demanded.

But the man wasn't interested in chatting us up, he just wanted Julia's autograph. Finally, at 10 P.M. on my forty-second birthday, Julia and I returned to our rooms and I went to bed alone. Again. It's all very well having the occasional shag with Tennis Man but going to bed on my own every night is getting very boring. I want a nice boyfriend to snuggle up to—a nice, rich boyfriend.

14

Royally Pissed Off

One of the Manila gigs was to be held in our hotel, the Makati Shangri-La. Very convenient indeed. It was to celebrate the first anniversary of Joey FM, the radio station that was promoting the minitour.

Because Julia is, as I get a kick out of saying, very big in the Philippines, she'd had loads of press coverage, including an MTV Asia special where they gave her sixth album, *The Collection,* a massive plug. Very frustrating, despite all the precious publicity, the record had already sold out in the stores so even if more people wanted to buy it, they couldn't.

This happens a lot in the music business and can be soul destroying for an artist. *The Collection* was just fourteen hundred records short of going gold in the Philippines. Which reminds me: What's the difference between God and an A & R man?

Answer: God doesn't think he's an A & R man.

So there we were, trying not to be too angry that the record wasn't even in the shops when I thought I'd pop out for a manicure and pedicure. "I'll only be half an hour," I said. An hour and a half later, I was greeted by a raised eyebrow: "I had to hold my own hair dryer, you know."

"Sorry about that," I said, "my nails look nice though. Guess what happened at the beauty salon? They thought I was you. No wonder everyone has been bowing and scraping to me since we arrived. It's because I act like a diva and you walk so slowly behind me."

Julia didn't look very happy. "Why don't you have an afternoon nap?" I suggested. She thanked me for my thoughtfulness, which I felt a bit bad about as my motives were entirely selfish. I could get my hair done while she slept. It would only take half an hour. I made it quite clear to the stylist that I didn't want it back-combed as that is ageing. He said with a flamboyant wave: "By the time I've finished you'll look like Kim Bassinger!"

Julia guffawed when I walked into her room. "Kim Bassinger? You look more like Princess Anne."* I was heartbroken. I should have known not to trust the stylist as all the staff in the salon were dressed in somber black and looked as if they were starring in *The Matrix*.

Joey FM had invited 2,500 people to the concert and ordered food for 1,800, working on the assumption that when you invite people to a party, only half show up. Not only did all 2,500 people turn up, they brought their friends and relatives with them to hear Julia sing. Four thousand people watched that concert. The hotel was able to feed an extra 1,500 with just half an hour's notice.

Another triumph. The chairman of the company that owns Joey FM invited us to dine with him. He was a charm-

---

* Her Majesty Queen Elizabeth II's middle-aged daughter who does much good work for charity but isn't gorgeous like her former sister-in-law, Princess Diana, and refuses to be photographed kissing babies so isn't revered in America. Something you'll never hear anyone say in the UK: "Doesn't Princess Anne's hair look great today?"

ing man and said that he often comes to LA on business, so we invited him to join us for afternoon tea at our little house by the beach. He said that he would take us to tea at the Bel Air. I said: "No, really, come to the house. The Bel Air is so expensive." This made him and his entourage laugh.

It turns out that he's the highest paid businessman in Asia and earns a million dollars a month. That's not including his stock options. He's also the president of a bank and has four bodyguards with him at all times. "Tea at the Bel Air it is then." I whispered to Julia, "Do you think he'd make a suitable second husband?"

Mention the Philippines to most Westerners and they just think of Imelda Marcos and her shoe collection. She is not a popular woman and many stories of her unreasonableness abound. We were told that when her husband, Ferdinand, was president in the early eighties, Imelda was overseeing the building of a huge convention center that she wanted completed before some VIP arrived for a state visit.

It's said that she prevented the rescue of fifteen construction workers who'd become trapped after a cave-in as it would have delayed the opening, so they were buried alive. But the convention center never opened at all as people refused to enter it believing it to be haunted by the dead workers.

Eventually the Marcos regime was overthrown in a bloodless coup. One of Julia's songs, "Invisible War," was the underground movement's anthem during the Marcos years, which is one of the reasons why Julia is so popular there. Another reason is that she gets lots of radio play in the Philippines and people will only buy the records that they are allowed to hear. It also helps to have them available in the shops.

15

Sick as a Dog

We missed the flight from Manila to the Philippine island of Cebu for the last gig because the traffic was worse than normal. I was not a happy bunny. Julia said: "Relax. This is all part of life on the road."

I said: "Being a road warrior is definitely starting to lose its appeal." We played "I Spy" in the VIP lounge as we waited for the next available flight.

Julia said: "You should think yourself lucky you aren't stuck in a tour bus as I was for months on end in the early days."

"My life wasn't exactly a picnic. I was up to my armpits in dirty nappies* and screaming babies. We didn't have disposable nappies in those days, you know," I said.

Later, as we swam in our own private lagoon outside the Tea Tree Cottage (mansion more like) in the fabulous Plantation Bay resort, I told Julia: "You must sign a new record deal and have a big hit single PDQ† because I do not want to give

---

* Diapers.
† Pretty Damn Quick.

up this luxury lifestyle. It suits me so very well, don't you think?"

In recognition of her divaness, Julia had the Presidential Suite. I didn't exactly feel like I was slumming it in the vice-presidential quarters. And we had our own butler on call 24 hours a day. Two of them worked 12-hour shifts. Lovely young ladies who responded to each summons speedily. Respectful but not servile. Nothing was too much trouble. Tea. Cake. Sew a button on. Laundry. We even had our own private nurse!

I advised Julia that she should keep thinking of the joy of servants and our own private lagoon as she sings "Love Moves In Mysterious Ways"—her least favorite but most popular song with Filipinos. "Small price to pay," I said. "Small price to pay."

The day we arrived in Cebu the weather was lovely. Then the rains came and they came and they came and brought with them all sorts of bugs and bacteria that made a beeline for Julia, and she was struck by a hideous gastric flu. She called it Filipino Plague. I called it Cebu Poo. I was sure we'd have to pull the gig but thanks to Dr. Theatre's "The Show Must Go On" attitude, positive affirmations (I radiate health and happiness. I radiate health and happiness), Imodium and ibuprofen, she played a blinder.★

We invited the Filipino band and the singers to our room for a singsong, peanuts and beer after the show. It was a wonderful, magical time. We didn't get to bed until 3:30 A.M. I felt like Keith Moon.

The Filipino Plague was back with vengeance the next day and Julia looked and felt as badly as she'd ever done in her life.

★ An excellent piece of play, usually in a football (soccer) game.

I was exhausted, having waited on Julia hand and foot during her illness, even staying up all night with her. I said: "No wonder so many artists go mad, drink too much, or take too many drugs. Life on the road and the relentless pressure to write hit singles is way too hard." Julia nodded.

I don't think I want Julia to be a full-time diva. Having tasted the diva treatment in the Philippines, it does seem to have its downside. No privacy. Constant staring from the public, with everyone wanting to be your best friend. The signing of autographs can be a gigantic pain in the arse when you've already signed five thousand.

Although Julia seems to do it with a happy heart and never looks bored when asked for the millionth time by a reporter: "Tell me, do you write the lyrics or the music first?" (Both at the same time.)

Julia was so sick we had to get a hotel room in Manila for an hour so she could lie down before the flight back to LA. She painted on a smile, signed another million autographs at the airport and, in between pukes, did a TV interview. I wanted to tell everyone to Sod Off but not my sister.

As David Crosby once told a reporter who wanted to know how he could justify his massive fee for an hour's performance: "We're not getting paid for that hour but the other twenty-three."

We queued up with our business class tickets to check-in and Julia signed more autographs and had her photograph taken with every member of the airport staff. Finally, a nice lady took our tickets and passports and said to Julia: "Welcome to Philippines Airlines. We are upgrading you and your sister to first class."

I looked up to the heavens and gave thanks. There is a God.

16

Birthday Boy

It was fantastic to be greeted by our sons when we arrived home after the Philippines trip. My son didn't keep licking my face as Julia's did, but he was very happy to see me.

Max was a beautiful, adorable child. I remember praying he'd be out of nappies by the time he went for his first job interview. He was.

I helped him practice and practice to overcome the worst clumsiness and become captain of the school football team.

I let him take the day off school and took him to London (we lived in Dorset at that time) to see Prince play at Earl's Court (The Arrowhead Pond, Anaheim), and he took my place as Julia's Plus One to see The Rolling Stones play at Wembley Arena (The Staples Center) (or was it Wembley Stadium?*).

I watched his triumphant performance as Ariel in All Saints Secondary School's production of *The Tempest*† after he had broken his neck the previous summer and spent two months in skull traction.

---

* Shea Stadium.
† William Shakespeare's play not made into a film by Kenneth Brannagh.

He flipped over the handlebars of his mountain bike when he tried to leap a small rock on his path. This was his last and most spectacular tumble. He coped with the injury and hospitalization with great wit and fortitude. I was assured by his doctors that Max would make a complete recovery so I wasn't too anxious and concentrated on helping him pass the time.

We played "I Spy" a lot, read heaps, and watched too much television. The nurses gave him a pair of prism glasses so he could watch TV from his prone position.

After the first ten days when Max wasn't so poorly and had settled into a routine, I stopped staying with him all his waking hours and split the shifts with his dad. I stayed with Max during the day and his dad took over in the evening.

Julia came straight down to Weymouth to see Max as soon as she stepped off a plane from Japan. The whole family rallied round. Julia brought her healing crystals for Max much to our brother, Mark's, amusement.

Mark got us into serious trouble with the ward Sister for disturbing the other patients when he took one of the crystals in his hand and held it up to the heavens.

"It's a miracle! I was overcome by the strongest itch in my anus. I took one of these mighty crystals and used its magical powers to scratch the anal area that was causing me so much discomfort. And lo, the itching ceased. Behold, I am cured!"

It wasn't all smiles during Max's ordeal. There were some very distressing moments. During the first week he was often sick, which involved carefully rotating him on his side so he didn't choke. It was horrific to watch. Max must have been petrified.

When you spend so much time flat on your back, you can hallucinate because the oxygen isn't getting to your brain. This happened to Max a couple of times. He thought he was covered in spiders, which was especially upsetting for me because I hate spiders.

He had to get used to walking again once he was out of the skull traction. He was always skinny but became emaciated after his confinement and it took him awhile to get moving again. He had to wear one of those head and neck braces for a month or so after he came out of skull traction. It really was a terrible ordeal for him but he never complained.

He's never looked back since. Well, he can't because it hurts his neck. Seriously, apart from the odd arthritic twinge when he gets cold or damp, he's tip-top.

I cried outside his bedroom door as I listened to him sing the first love song he wrote for his first girlfriend. I still cry every time he sings it.

I eventually forgave him after he disobeyed me by having a party that lasted for two weeks while I was visiting Julia in California. I distinctly remember saying as I walked out the front door: "Don't have any parties." I've since learned that there were teenagers sitting on the roof and puking in the garden. The music was so loud the neighbors called the police.

He apologized for the damage and for disobeying me but said that he didn't regret it because it was the best time he'd ever had in his life. The "two week party incident" as I still refer to it was the only time I've ever been mad at him.

Julia said at the time: "It's your own bloody fault for thinking a seventeen-year-old teenager who sees himself as the next Kurt Cobain could be trusted to do anything else." She wouldn't have been as understanding if she'd seen the state his friends had left her bedroom in.

I found out later that the blood had come from the foot of one of the little shits who'd cut himself as he'd stepped on and then broken a porcelain toilet roll holder in a failed attempt to hoist himself through the bathroom window and onto the roof.

Anyway, I've laughed and cried with him through good films and bad. We shared a bottle of eighteen-year-old Margaux on his eighteenth birthday and here we are in California about to celebrate his twenty-first. My baby. My boy.

He didn't want to go to a fancy restaurant (phew!) but to have a dinner at home. He chose the menu and invited the guests. Steak followed by apple pie.

As we drank champagne and toasted his health, I asked each guest around the dinner table to give Max a piece of advice they wished they'd had when they were twenty-one. My favorites were:

"Be fearless and live your dreams."

"Always wear a condom."

"Always take Beverly Glen."★

"Always wear a condom when taking Beverly Glen."

The hardest thing for a mother to do is to gently tip her children out of the nest knowing that they will face many painful experiences in the big scary world without you there to pick up the pieces and make everything better.

It's probably best to move to another continent so it won't be so easy for them to move back in with you when the going gets too tough, as it surely will.

We had tears of laughter rolling down our faces the next day when he finished reading me the e-mail that he'd received from his eighty-three-year-old paternal grandmother. It said:

Happy Birthday.
How is my boy?

★ LA Street, not an American daytime television program or local girl.

Your Dad told me he thought you were gay at one time BUT NOT
NOW.
I told him "He is my boy. He is not gay."
He said you put on silly hats that make you look like that.
PLEASE, PLEASE DON'T put on those hats.
Take care and look after yourself.
You are and always will be "my boy."
I love you.
Your Grandma

I managed to hold back the tears as I waved Max off at
the airport until he was out of sight. We Brits don't like public displays of emotion. I miss not seeing him and his sister
every day. Twice a week would be perfect.

17

Bum Rap

Following my triumphant performance as Julia's "assister" in the Philippines, I am to be trusted with more responsibility, namely, guitar roadie. I can carry three guitars at a time and a guitar stand in my mouth, so it only takes two trips to the car to unload everything.

First day on the job and Julia is recording a demo at The Village in West LA. I arrive after her with the guitars and struggle from the car. As I fall through the door I spit the guitar stand out of my mouth and gasp: "Why don't you stick a brush up my arse, then I can sweep the floor as well."

She is in no mood for humor. "You've brought the wrong guitar. I couldn't have been more clear that you should bring the Collings and the Martin, not the Ferrington."

I said: "I'm so used to packing the Martin and the Ferrington for the live gigs at Largo that I must have been running on automatic pilot. Forgive me. I am an idiot. You were indeed quite clear in your instruction. I assure you that I will take my responsibility more seriously in future."

I thought: "I think you might be confusing me with someone who gives a shit. Perhaps you might like to pack your own guitars from now on." She used to hero-worship me when she was seven and carried MY bags!

Another thing that I keep getting wrong is losing the bottom part of the guitar stands when we leave the gigs. It comes out for easy packing and I somehow lose them on the way back from the venue. We now have five stands that are totally useless because that vital bottom part is missing.

When it looked as if I had lost a sixth one, Julia was not pleased. Even I was beginning to think that I might be useless until I found the missing part in Muttley's apartment with most of the plastic chewed off. And guess what? It wasn't such a big deal when she realized that Muttley was the villain of the piece.

I've been feeling a bit sorry for the Muttster. He's feeling violated since the dog groomer "expressed his anus." This— the dog groomer told us with a straight face—is done to ensure that the area doesn't get infected, which happens because dogs often lick their anus after having just licked another dog's bottom, which may also be infected because other owners aren't as conscientious in the cleanliness department as we are.

And he's got an ear infection. The vet showed us how to get his ear drops in, but Muttley wouldn't let us do it. The third and final attempt ended in tears with the canine nearly biting Julia's hand off (slight exaggeration) and that was with a muzzle on! I refused to be beaten by a bloody dog and did a victory dance when I got some drops in at 3 A.M. while he slept. He now sleeps with one eye open so it is impossible to take him by surprise again.

In the end we had to have him admitted to the veterinary hospital and they recommended a course of antibiotics. The drugs cost $161.42! That ear infection cost over a thousand bucks.

We don't call it the "vets" any more as he runs a mile at the mention of the word. We call it summer camp. Boy does that dog have abandonment issues.

I said to Julia: "I reckon he's cost about $6,000 so far and he's only eight months!"

"And he's worth every penny," she said as she cuddled him on the sofa. "Suzanne took a $10,000 bank loan to pay for Mary The Pit Bull's chemotherapy after she had a cancerous tumor removed from her foot."

"Madness," I said. "Utter madness."

Things have not been going well since we got back from the Philippines. Tennis Man told me that he didn't want to jeopardize our friendship by getting emotionally involved and wants to be just friends. I didn't bother saying that I didn't want to get emotionally involved either, just have sex once a fortnight, because I knew that what he meant was that he'd met someone more suitable.

A week later, after he missed an easy volley at the net, Tennis Man casually mentioned that he had met someone. I feigned surprise and delight for him. She's just fifteen (yes, fifteen) years younger than me and he thinks she might be "the one." 15-Love!

Julia listened sympathetically as I groaned: "So my fuck buddy ended up being fucking useless. Fucking typical."

But there is some good news. Mum and Dad are coming to visit and Mum likes dogs even less than I do.

18

Mum's the Word

We've rented an SUV (we call it the parent mobile) as Mum and Dad can't get in and out of the Mustang. It's not easy getting three guitars, stands, leads, the gigantic "gig bag," and a dog in and out of a saucy little sports car either, so I think the Mustang's days may be numbered.

Also, when we park outside the house, it's so low and the pavement is so uneven that we can't open the passenger door. Every time we park we say we're going to get rid of it, but it's great to drive and we get lots of looks from cute guys when we drive along Sunset Boulevard with the roof down and our baseball caps on to protect us from the sun. Since we read that Kim Bassinger even covers her face when she walks from the house to the car to protect herself from the evil, ageing sun, we have been taking every precaution.

Julia and I have been preparing for Mum and Dad's trip for some time. Julia said: "I want everything to be perfect. The last time they came I made some fatal errors. I thought they'd enjoy my healthy diet of fish and vegetables."

"The poor old buggers were gagging for carbohydrates. They need meat and two veg and lots of cake!" I said.

Julia continued: "What with the enormity of the struggle

to get in and out of the Mustang and Mum's travel sickness, the trip was a bit of a disaster. But all this was BC (Before Claire), and you know how to feed them. Everything will be fine so long as we never look at each other or up to heaven if Mum says something that only a Mum can say."

I agreed: "We'll agree with everything either parent says, however controversial, and everything will be hunky."

Mum and Dad have been married for forty-five years. I know that Mum was a virgin on her wedding night, but I don't know if she likes sex because we have never discussed the subject. I know that Dad loves Mum because he painted it on our living room wall with emulsion when we were children. "Roy loves Muriel," it said in giant letters. It would be revealed every few years when Dad stripped off the wallpaper to redecorate. The best thing a man can do for his children is to love their mother.

Dad was an underwater photographer with the Ministry of Defense. Mum was a traditional housewife. She dusted to make sure there never was any dust and she cooked us a hot meal every night whether she felt like it or not. She never complained and was only sick once when I was about sixteen and she had to have an ovary removed. The thing I admire most about Mum is that she never shouted at us when we were kids. Although she did raise her voice once when I was eleven and asked her for the hundredth time why I couldn't go camping on the beach with some friends and no adult supervision.

Dad is the clown who makes us laugh all the time, but Mum is the heartbeat of our family. Dad delivered Julia. Mum had gone into labor but the midwife, Nurse Stanley, had gone to the next village to lance a boil, so Mum and Dad handled everything themselves. They didn't have mobile phones or pagers. Not even a phone in the house.

Mark was born at home as well. I didn't hear a thing during his or Julia's delivery, so Mum must have been biting on a stick—no epidurals or pethadine in those days. Mind you, they didn't have epidurals in Dorset when Max was born either. There was much huffing and puffing and screaming for mercy as I recall. Most of the screaming came from Max's father as I bit down on his arm.

I was born in St. Mary's Hospital, Portsmouth. Men weren't present during births then, so Dad was sent home and told to call in the morning. He stayed at his parents' house in Southsea as it was nearer the hospital.

Nanny Fordham, Grandpa, and Uncle George stood outside their small terraced house as Dad cycled up the road to use the call box to find out if his baby had been born. He cycled back down Bath Road with both hands straight up in the air, the sign that it was a girl. Nan told me years later that he was beaming from ear to ear and everyone on the street cheered and clapped.

Dad used to cycle to work at Portsmouth Dockyard every day. Every time I moaned about Dad to Mum, which wasn't often, she'd remind me about the time he cycled four miles in heavy winds and rain, balancing a huge doll's house for me on the crossbar.

She's clearly forgotten the time when I was three and she'd sent me to see how Dad was getting on wallpapering the hallway. I was able to report that I'd heard him mumble: "It's like trying to hang lumps of shit." Dad is often in trouble with Mum for saying or doing the wrong thing, but she is the first to defend him if anyone else criticizes him.

Mum and Dad are great but need a cup of tea and a snack every hour and want to know while we are still eating lunch what we're having for dinner. Julia and I arranged for them to stay on the next street at a friend's vacant apartment, so we wouldn't get under each other's feet and on each other's nerves. There's only one bathroom in our little house so it would have been chaos in the mornings. We spend the days and evenings together.

Just when you think nothing will ever surprise you again in your life, Mum fell in love with Muttley on sight. This is a woman who still walks everywhere, head bowed, with her eyes firmly on the pavement constantly on the lookout for dog muck. Woe-betide anyone who gets any canine excrement on her carpet. Needless to say, I was always treading in doggy do as a child and traipsing it through the house.

I asked Mum: "Why did you make me wear those awful plastic Jelly shoes? They were a magnet to dog poo. It was almost impossible to scoop the poop from the corrugated soles."

She said: "But I did, didn't I? Over and over again. And I don't think you ever heard me complain about it. By the way, your tea towels need boiling." And then she carried on talking to Muttley like he was a favorite grandchild. Dad took photographs of anything and everything on his new digital camera. "Quiet please, this is a silent film." He says that every time he takes a photograph.

We held a small gathering in Mum and Dad's honor at the house and I was persuaded to sing a duet with Julia. After a lot of arm twisting and two glasses of Chateau Neuf Du Pape, I agreed to sing "Big Yellow Taxi." We'd never sung it together in front of anyone else before.

I was so overcome by the whooping and cheering of the audience that when it came to the bit where Julia (or Her Holiness Joni Mitchell) sings "Late at night I heard a screen door slam" and I do my "slam slam" backing vocal, I got a bit carried away with my arm movements and punched Julia in the eye, rendering her unconscious. She was unable to continue, but I basked in the adulation and promised after much pleading from those lucky enough to witness my rare performance that I would indeed perform in public again.

Julia's black eye cleared up after ten days and there was no swelling after five, so I don't know why she made such a fuss.

Mum is so convinced we'll end up as old maids that she asks the marital status of any man we meet. Julia brought home a friend of a friend she'd bumped into on Main Street. He wanted to see our home as its quaintness is renowned. Well, of course, as soon as Mum had discreetly ascertained that he was single (17 seconds), she invited him to take tea with us in the garden.

"What do you do for a living?" she asked.

He said: "I'm an artist."

"What sort of artist?"

"I specialize in figurative nudes."

"You should paint Claire," said Mum. "She looks slimmer with her clothes off."

I was so shocked I forgot our pact, looked up to heaven and at Julia and shook my head in disbelief.

19

Star Attractions

The news in America is appalling. Not that nothing happens, it's the way they report it and what they think is newsworthy that beggars belief. Only very rarely do national television companies mention a story outside America. The stories the program editors choose to lead with here are astonishing.

The local California news running order goes something like this:

1. It rained today.
2. How to keep your Christmas tree moist.
3. John Travolta has a new hairstyle.
4. Four children die in a house fire (even if they've got pictures of the flames!).

Mind you, the UK's not far behind. George Clooney leaving *ER* made the front page of the *Guardian* but that was pretty big news. Although I am a news snob, it didn't stop me from accepting an assignment from Associated Press TV to cover the *Vanity Fair* Oscar party.

Moira and Suzanne assumed that I was going to be mingling with the stars inside Morton's but I was actually penned in a confined space outside with the rest of the press pack, jostling for position and screaming at all the celebrities to come and talk to us.

Michael Caine was charming as was Phil Collins and Billy Connolly and Bridget Fonda. Robin Williams, bless him, spoke to anyone who asked. I also interviewed two men who were clutching Oscars despite having absolutely no idea who they were. I eventually worked out that one of them must have been the guy who wrote *The Cider House Rules* and the other wrote the best original score.

I can report that Keanu Reeves is gorgeous in the flesh. James Woods is very odd and I sincerely hope that the four stunning but dim-looking young women draped over Hugh Hefner are getting paid an awful lot of money to have sex with him. No wonder Heff's walking so slowly and with a limp these days.

I almost came to blows with a reporter from an obscure cable channel who claimed that I was in her space. She was so busy marking out her territory with chalk that she missed Sidney Poitier. Ha!

I may be forced to get a regular job soon as money is going out a lot faster than it's coming in. I don't think my credit cards can take the strain of California living for much longer. While I don't feel bad using Julia's money for house-hold items as I am chief cook and bottle washer, I use my own money for personal stuff like the kids' and my flights.

I'm afraid the odd phone report for ITN and the Annual Oscar Fest aren't generating enough cash. The chances of me getting even a night shift in an LA newsroom are slim to none and (surprise, surprise) there aren't any job offers in the, who *Hollywood Reporter* and *Variety* insist that "applicants must be at least forty."

A recent trip to the LA Museum of Contemporary Art

makes me think I could make a career as a contemporary artist. There are "works of art" hanging there that are indeed priceless.

One woman specializes in randomly writing numbers in pencil on pieces of graph paper. There are canvases with one brush stroke. Plain orange canvases. Red ones. Yellow ones. Piles of bricks. Planks of wood. Pieces of poo.

I said to Julia: "This lunacy isn't confined to LA. I've seen the same bollocks masquerading as art in London, New York, and Paris." The Getty Museum is largely crap free though.

I was having lunch with Moira and Suzanne last week at Pannecotta in Westwood. (They serve terrific salads and an excellent mushroom risotto.) We discussed in some detail the new fad to have collagen pumped into your lips to eradicate fine lines. "Isn't it crazy that some vegetarian women won't eat a hamburger but don't mind having cow fat injected into their lips?" said Moira.

I added: "I'm told it's especially popular with hookers whose mouths are constantly puckered from giving so many blow jobs. I guess puffing on cigarettes probably has the same effect. But it isn't so pleasurable for men."

Suzanne said wearily: "I tell you, too many blow jobs does make your jaw ache. For our first Christmas I gave one ex boyfriend "The 12 Blow Jobs of Christmas" as one of his gifts."

"Excuse me?"

"Every day for twelve days I dressed up in a different sexy Christmassy outfit and gave him a blow job. A snowflake one day. A fairy. An angel, and so on."

"Including Christmas Day?" I asked

She nodded. "And he never even proposed."

I wondered aloud: "What's a girl gotta do?"

Which reminds me of the little girl who walked past her

parents' bedroom and witnessed her mother performing that same sexual favor. She was a very inquisitive but polite child and thoughtfully did not interrupt the proceedings.

Later, after her father had left for work, she asked her mother if that was what you did to get pregnant. To which the mother replied: "No, honey. That's what you do to get jewelry."

Talking of sex, I have finally met a man here who moves my meter. He is handsome, funny as hell, and forty-something. We were chatting over a hamburger at the Holly-wood Manager's house. We got on incredibly well. He's a writer and could be most suitable. He was definitely flirta-tious until this truly stunning young girl breezed in.

She was gorgeous. It soon became apparent that she was there at the Writer's invitation and he was clearly fascinated by this woman. The rest of our party sat captivated by the beautiful yet needy creature as she shared her life story with us. She had broken up with her lover the night before (big grin on the Writer's face). She looked twenty-two but was ac-tually, unbelievably, thirty and had two children by different fathers.

Her previous relationship, she explained to the mesmer-ized guests, had broken up after she found out that her boy-friend had slept with her mother. I didn't feel I knew the Writer well enough to tell him to run for the hills and si-lently hoped that he would see the danger signs before too much emotional damage was done and come knocking at my door.

20

Muttley Rules

"You cannot be serious," I said.

Julia said: "I don't see why not. Sheryl Crow and Shawn Colvin take their pets on the road with them when they tour so why can't I take Muttley?"

"Because he is out of control," I said, "and capable of eating a tour bus and its contents."

"He doesn't like it when we leave him. I'll get him trained."

"Good luck."

The New Dog Trainer was more concerned that Muttley had snapped at me a couple of times when I'd tried to move him off the sofa than with his refusal to come when called unless he feels like it. She says she can also stop him barking at the postman and the FedEx lady. I told her: "It's not an exaggeration to say that sometimes I feel as if I'm starring in *The Hound of the Baskervilles.*"

All this will be done for the princely sum of $700 for a seven-week course that we'd be welcome to pay in advance. I couldn't stay in the room while the Dog Trainer asked Julia about Muttley's history. "Jesus. You'd think he was applying to study medicine at Harvard," I said.

It would appear that the reason Muttley does occasionally respond to commands is that he is a dog who wants to please but he is clearly not a trained dog. I said to Julia: "I could have told you that for nothing."

The Dog Trainer also felt that if we don't take him with us when we go away we shouldn't get someone to move into the house to take care of him because that will make him depressed! In future, she suggested, we should send him to Paradise Ranch, a country club for dogs in Sun Valley. "They'll even collect the dog from you and bring him back. They are not caged up but roam the ranch freely and are blissfully happy there. This way Muttley will not feel that he has been abandoned but that he too is having a vacation," she said.

"Marvelous," said Julia, "how much is it and when can we book him in?"

"It's not simply a case of paying up and booking him in. The owners will want to interview Muttley before they will let him stay there," she said.

The con artist, I'm sorry, "animal behaviorist," also recommended that we stop taking him to the dog park in Venice. "You don't get a very good class of dog there. The dog park on the Strand and 6th is much more suitable."

The Dog Trainer is an Amazonian blonde, around my age, very upright. I think she'd buff up with a bit of lippie and mascara but clearly prefers a natural look. She gets straight to the point. No time for small talk. Firm but fair. Not to be messed with.

There was just time for her to show us how to do Muttley's homework before she had to go to see her next sucker, I mean client. "Taking the treat, we must call him by his name in a kindly voice being careful to repeat the command when he has arrived in front of us, then we reward him with the said treat. If we do that seventy times a day for a week he'll soon get the message," she said.

"Seventy?"

"Seventy."

And another sixty times a day we must make him "sit" on command and reward him with a treat.

"He'll be the size of a horse after all those treats," I said.

Then she made ME take part in the charade as the dog must also learn to respond to my commands. She said: "I'm sensing your negativity towards Muttley. And if I can sense it, so can Muttley. It's vital that you get into the spirit of things and speak to him in a kindly tone."

I said: "The money this dog has cost so far would have been much better spent trying to find a cure for cancer or eradicating Third World debt." I'm sure I saw hatred in Julia's eyes. And guess who had to dog sit while Julia went out on a date with her new gentleman caller? At least he brought a smile to her face.

21

Action!

I am overjoyed. I've been offered a job in a movie that My George is thinking about starring in. I have the grand title of "Artist's Liaison." I won't be getting paid. It's for the experience. I deserve a Golden Globe for the way I so casually received the news that I might at last meet my beloved George.

Judith told me. She's got a part in the film and, apparently, her husband, who's written and is directing it, knows George and has sent him the script.

I have been practicing how I will greet George the first time we meet. A nod of the head so slight he'll think I hadn't even noticed him? A great big bear hug perhaps? A firm handshake and slap on the back? The suspense is killing me.

I was told that George wouldn't make his decision on whether to take the part until the last minute, so you can imagine my excitement when I overheard the director telling one of the producers as I arrived for the first read through of the script how thrilled he was that George was on board.

I raced for the rest room to check my makeup and practice my reaction when My George and I were finally introduced. I took a sharp intake of breath as the director called out "Hey, Claire, come and meet George." I could see the director but My George was hidden behind two other actors.

I met George all right. George Wendt (Norm in *Cheers*). George Clooney did *O Brother, Where Art Thou?* instead. To rub salt into the wound, making a movie isn't as glamorous as you might think. I did get to wear a walkie-talkie headset, which made me feel quite important but there is so much hanging around in boiling temperatures that at times it was unbearable.

I told Julia as I lay exhausted on the sofa: "I am being ordered about by girls half my age and at one point was called upon to remove some dog shit that an actor was about to step in."

She said: "Lucky for you we carry a plastic bag with us at all times and are always prepared for such an eventuality."

I said: "You might think it's lucky, but I think it's a sad reflection on my life that I can clean up dog shit at a moment's notice."

The next day on set, which I spent fetching and carrying for the world and her sister, the props man apologized for shouting at me for getting his Starbucks coffee order wrong. He said: "Don't take any notice of me. I'm a Capricorn from New York." I'm sure Moira will have something to say about that.

Things could be worse. I could be an actor. They have to sit around for hours in their trailer until they are called for makeup and wardrobe and then wait a few more hours to be called to the set. They wait in such good humor that they must be acting.

Judith isn't very happy either. She'd been understandably nervous during her first scene. She sat at a table with old pros Ken Mars (he played the Nazi who wrote "Springtime for

Hitler" in the movie version of *The Producers*) and Bob Einstein (his brother Albert didn't think he'd be taken seriously as an actor with a name like Albert Einstein so changed it to Albert Brooks).

Judith didn't have any lines but had to look interested and enjoy her afternoon tea while Ken Mars was talking. The director shook his head and shouted: "Cut! Let's do that again. We're not making a film about choosing a sandwich." If there had been an Oscar for "Most Dramatic Choosing of a Sandwich," Jude would have won it.

Being in the movie industry is far too much like hard work. I've got blisters on my feet and my legs ache from running to the set and back to base camp. The hanging around waiting for action in sweltering heat is exhausting. Poor George Wendt looks like he's going to keel over.

As I'm not getting paid, I didn't feel too bad about taking a sickie. Julia said I was being unprofessional.

I said: "You wouldn't be saying that if the second AD gave your walkie-talkie to an intern so you were effectively incommunicado on set and didn't have a clue what was going on. It might sound petty to you but having my walkie-talkie taken away was very upsetting."

Julia said: "If you do get a credit at the end of the film at all, it will say Claire Fordham Artist's Liaison Part-Time or When She Felt Like It."

I've been asked by Granada TV to work as a fixer for Michael Nicholson who's in tinsel town to do a 15-minute piece for *Tonight With Trevor McDonald:* "How Hollywood Rewrites History." Mike is the correspondent whose heroic effort to bring a little girl into the UK from war torn Bosnia inspired the film *Welcome to Sarajevo*.

Ironically, the previous evening I'd been playing "Celebrity" with Woody Harrelson who starred in the film. I'm not a friend of his but he's a friend of our next-door neighbor, Jennifer, who was hosting the party and he used to live on our street. Coincidence? You be the judge.

Mike Nicholson and his producer met me at the English pub, The Cock and Bull, to watch England beat Germany 1-0 in the European Cup. In the best English tradition we went out for a slap-up lunch to celebrate our team's victory, despite the fact that England didn't play very well. Expense accounts are wonderful things.

While I've been making my splash in the movies, Muttley has been quite sickly. The poor little bugger has been X rayed and prodded in private places (at great expense obviously) by a host of vets who've diagnosed his condition as colitis, which, they believe, was probably brought on by stress.

I've heard it all now. Julia explained: "His strict training regime has got him in such a tizzy that his colon has become ulcerated."

They kept him in hospital for three days during which time he pulled out and ate his catheter and intravenous drip.

I said: "Eating the condom must have given him a taste for plastic."

"Don't be nasty," said Julia. "All the vets love him. They say he's their favorite."

I said: "Of course they love him. He must be their biggest source of revenue. I expect by the time Muttley's fifteen, he'll have earned all the partners enough money to put their children through college."

I'm beginning to feel quite sorry for him. I said: "Can't you send a note to his Nazi Dog Trainer asking if he can be excused until he's better?"

"No," Julia said. "He's making such good progress. And stop calling the trainer a Nazi."

The Nice Trainer has instructed Julia to buy six large

water sprayers and six small ones. The large ones will be filled with water and sprayed at the delinquent dog if he barks at the postman or eats something that he shouldn't.

The Nice Trainer explained: "The small ones will be filled with foul tasting liquid like bitter apple, which will be sprayed into his mouth if he growls at anyone."

I whispered to Julia: "Let's stop pussyfooting around and cut off his testicles. Oh! I forgot. We already have."

He has finally responded to a command. He came when Julia called him and she rewarded him, not with a dog biscuit but the fresh salmon I was saving for my supper. I was outraged. "Jesus, you'd think he'd won a bloody Golden Globe," I said.

22

Move Away from the Honeypot

The Writer called and left a message. I'd almost given up on him. He said that he'd enjoyed meeting me at the Hollywood Manager's house because I'm such fun and he would love to see me again, so I invited him to one of Judith's afternoon tea parties. He cancelled his plans and came with me. Everyone thought he was hilarious and said we looked perfect together. Moira quickly established that he is a Taurus and whispered to me that this was a good thing what with me being a Pisces.

I said: "Then how come Julia, who's a Leo, is so suited to her new gentleman caller and he's a Taurus as well?"

Moira said: "Because they have the same moon rising." This from a woman who thinks that all Virgos are perverts.

The Writer called two days later to say he'd enjoyed himself at the tea, so I invited him to dinner at Naomi's house. We drove to the Hollywood Hills in the Mustang. Julia sat in the back with Muttley and her gentleman caller while the Writer sat in the front with me, his knees practically touching his chin he was so cramped in our little sports car.

He complained all the way there and even more on the way home when it was our turn to sit in the back with the dog. He called again two days later to say that he'd had a surprisingly good time (I see a pattern forming with this calling every two days) and that he would like to take me out to dinner later in the week.

He mentioned that he took the beautiful yet needy creature out to dinner after the barbecue at the Hollywood Manager's house but said that the evening had not been a success because she kept flirting outrageously with the waiter and left him with an enormous bar bill. He's written an article this week extolling the virtues of voluptuous women over thin ones and called for an end to the current obsession with skinny women. There is a God.

Then I didn't hear from him for a week and when we did finally go out to dinner, I had to pay because his credit card was rejected. He blamed his bank. Hmm.

Later, while Julia and I were power walking along the beach to take my mind off the Writer date debacle and the disappointment that I may have attracted yet another pauper, she said: "The Nice Trainer was absolutely right. You do get a much better class of dog at the park on Strand. There's a Doberman there called Isabel who loves Muttley. Satan, the Rottweiler, at the Venice park looks at Muttley as if he's a McDonald's Happy Meal. She was wrong about one thing though. Muttley did manage to remove his new muzzle. She said that in all her years as a dog trainer she had never seen a dog get one off."

"Well, she has now," I said and felt quite proud of the hound.

The Nice Trainer has also given in on another issue. Muttley will not have bitter apple sprayed into his mouth if he growls. "All bad behavior is to be punished by squirting water right in between his eyes," Julia said.

I said: "If only I'd thought about using water sprays when I was training my children."

The water sprays have been dotted around the house for easy access. Perhaps surprisingly, I am against the idea but Julia insists I use them if Muttley barks.

I said: "I think I'll have holsters made for easier access. Go on punk. Make my day."

I have been surprised by how determined Julia is to see this training thing through. The first time she squirted him after he barked at the postman, he looked quite stunned. Even though he can't talk, you could see he was thinking: "What the fuck . . ."

Julia said: "Once you've shot him between the eyes, you have to follow up with lots of loves and a treat."

"Not confusing at all to the dog, I'm sure," I said.

It suddenly dawned on me while I was driving to Wild Oats on Wilshire for some soup and sushi that in the two weeks since I've been dating the Writer he hasn't actually taken me out on a date yet.

And, frankly, his constant jokes at the expense of the English are beginning to irritate. He's Scottish. His joy when Romania scored a penalty against us in the final minutes and booted us out of the European Cup knew no bounds. He said: "I was surprised that I did actually feel quite sorry for England at the final whistle, but it only lasted a nanosecond and may have been motivated by my desire to see them gubbed* by Italy in the next round."

I asked: "Aren't you being a tad hypocritical and disloyal to the Nationalist cause to be involved with a woman from the wrong side of the border?"

He said: "It's okay so long as you accept that the Scots are the master race and the English are colonial oppressors." I groaned.

* Stuffed. Beaten. Hammered.

He added: "Once a studio snaps up one of my screenplays for half a million dollars, I'll be quite a catch you know."

I don't think this Sassenach★ will be around to enjoy the benefit. As the last man I dated forgot his wallet both times we went out, I am determined that the next man I get involved with will at least call when he says he will and be able to afford to buy me dinner.

To this end, I readily agreed to accompany Julia as her Plus One to a party in Bel Air, but being rich and successful isn't enough if he doesn't make you laugh. I swear my eyes glazed over after five minutes listening to two wealthy men tell me about cochlear implants and the theory of chaos.

I said to Julia: "Is it too much to ask that a solvent, attractive, interesting man ask me out on a date?" She, by the way, is being courted by a handsome, successful, interesting man who clearly adores her. He's a sound engineer and produces records for small independent bands, which means small recording budgets. Cred, not bread.

"I've told you a million times before (exaggeration). Don't let them put their sausage in your honey pot until you really get to know them. It doesn't take long for a man to reveal his true self," Julia said smugly.

I will not let him put his sausage in my honey pot. I will not let him put his sausage in my honey pot. I will not let him put his sausage in my honey pot.

★ Original Anglo-Saxon person.

23

May the Best Man Win

Having been bored to death by two rich men at the Beverly Hills party, I ignored the voice of reason in my head and agreed to see the Writer again.

I was so nervous getting ready for my date that I plucked out every eyebrow hair except the white one that I was after. Julia assured me that the bald patch didn't show at all thanks to my cunning use of eyebrow pencil.

The Writer arrived on time and with a bunch of flowers, which looked very much like the ones in Moira's garden. I told him how I'd had great fun that afternoon playing with a kid's massive water spray gun at the swimming pool I use occasionally. "It fulfilled my fantasy to be Linda Hamilton in *Terminator 2*," I said.

He took me straight to Toys "R" Us and I bought two huge water guns so we could have a play fight at some later date. He said he'd get them but took far too long fumbling for his wallet and there was a long line of impatient people behind us. We called each other Bonnie and Clyde. Our first proper date and already we had pet names for each other!

We ate at the Border Grill and I promised him that I

wouldn't eat there with anyone else. We snogged on Santa Monica Pier.

That's what I call a date. He did not try to put his sausage in my honey pot.

While I was dreaming about My George the next morning, Julia brought me in my tea and toast as she does every day. "Did you let him put his sausage in your honey pot?" she asked.

"How did you know I was dreaming about My George?"

"I mean the Writer."

"No, I did not," I said proudly.

The Writer called the next day to say that he'd had a wonderful time and we saw each other again that night. I cooked dinner. He suggested we watch the Neville Brothers sing at the summer weekly free concert on Santa Monica Pier. Then we went for a walk on the beach in our bare feet and kissed on the sand. I felt like I was starring in *From Here to Eternity.*

The date went so well that he waited a week to call, but he did invite me out again. Julia said I was mad to go. "I'm going so I can tell him to his face why I think he's an arsehole and why I won't be seeing him again."

Rather confusingly, the date with the Writer went very well and I soon realized that I may have judged him harshly and prematurely. We both agreed that *The Patriot* was a pile of predictable shit but that Jason Isaacs was an excellent baddie. I said: "Why does every character Mel Gibson play hate the English so much?"

The Writer said: "That's perfectly understandable. Colonial oppressors, remember."

Despite his bigotry, the Writer is hilariously funny and smart and beguiling and entertaining. I was totally mesmerized. There were tears of laughter rolling down my face as he told me about the time he went to visit his dying father in hospital having been estranged from him for many years to be told by the nurse as he was leaving that he'd been baring his soul to the wrong patient.

He told me this joke: A woman was lying in her hospital bed having just given birth to her second baby. An unbearable snob from Bel Air in the next bed said: "When I had my first baby my husband bought me a Porsche."

The woman said: "That's nice."

The snob said: "When I had my second baby my husband bought me a house in the country."

"That's nice," said the woman.

"He's buying me a villa in the south of France as a thank you for this one," said the snob.

The woman said: "That's nice."

"Tell me, did your husband buy you anything after the birth of your first born?" asked the snob.

"Yes, he did as a matter of fact. He bought me elocution lessons."

"Really. And have you found them useful?"

"Yes, I have. I used to say fuck off, now I say that's nice."

We walked back to the car at 4:30 A.M. I've never stayed out so late in my life. I've never laughed so much. He kissed me in the doorway of the electric light shop. He said: "You're quite a good kisser. In fact I think it squeezed into my top three snogs of all time."

He wasn't fazed when I told him I was going back to England to see my two grown-up children and asked if he could see me when I got back.

I thought: "Why would I want to see you again you frugal, bigoted, selfish, narcissist?"

I said: "Okay."

The next day Muttley was put through his paces by the

Nice Trainer in lesson number three. She told us how important it is to say "no" like you mean it. She said: "Pardon my French, but when you say no it has to be more like FUCK YOU, YOU PIECE OF SHIT." This she growled in a voice so scary it was a Darth Vader meets Linda Blair in *The Exorcist* combo. She said: "Dogs like to know who is boss and they need boundaries."

Julia is flying to England a few days later than I as she doesn't want to miss the Fourth of July celebrations here in LA. I said: "Having just watched an American audience cheer every time Mel Gibson hacked an Englishman to pieces, I suggest you keep a very low profile or you might get lynched from the highest tree."

24

Anarchy Rules

The flight to London to be reunited with Max and Mia was surprisingly pleasing because, unusually, I sat next to someone interesting, another Brit living in California. She lives only two blocks away from me and it turned out that we have many acquaintances in common.

Cards were exchanged and we promised to do lunch. I'm becoming so LA! When I say we exchanged cards I mean she gave me hers and I tore a corner off the duty free magazine in the seat in front of me and wrote my number on that.

Max was at Terminal 3 to meet me. How I love that boy. I mean man. I was unable to resist commenting that his new haircut made him look like a convict and his clothes smelled of cigarette smoke. Oh my God! I have turned into my mother.

But that wasn't the first thing I said to him. The first thing I said was: "You look thinner than ever. Are you eating properly? Do you remember the time I gave you five pounds to buy ingredients to make yourself some lunch and you bought a bag of oven chips and twenty Benson and Hedges?" I saw him out of the corner of my eye look up to heaven and I raced back to customs so that I could restart our reunion on a better note.

He told me that his housemates saved ten pounds each by not going to a hairdresser and shaving each others' heads with dog clippers. Then I upset him again by insisting we take a cab and not the tube. He'd already bought the tube tickets and was appalled at, what he called, the unnecessary extravagance of a taxi.

I asked: "As someone with matching red Kipling luggage that Julia lent me, do I look like a person who takes the tube? I'll be paying for the cab anyway." He mumbled something about the evil of capitalism and, I noticed, he called the cab driver "mate."

What's happened to my son while I've been away? I later discovered that he was irritable because he had been misquoted in an interview for the *Socialist Worker** about the aforementioned evil of capitalism, which had been accompanied by a particularly unflattering photograph of him taken at a recent anticapitalist march in London. I doubted that it could be worse than his passport photograph but he said that it was.

I was quite surprised that the fruit of my loins was a placard carrying, marching anarchist, as I've always been a bit of a sit-on-the-fence social democrat. "Doesn't running your own record company make you a capitalist?" I asked.

He gave me a "don't go there" look and said: "All profits will be shared 50-50 with the artists."

"I think it's terrific that you are an independent thinker and a compassionate human being," I said. Once again I saw him look to the heavens with a look of bitter disappointment, or was it disdain?

Some friends from ITN lent me their apartment in Battersea and their car as they were on holiday in Australia.

* Weekly mouthpiece of the UK proletariat.

Max's girlfriend lives just around the corner so she joined us for dinner.

When Max went to the bathroom she said:"Don't go and see his house as it might upset you. It should be declared a serious health hazard by the local council. I don't think the toilet and bath have been cleaned once since Max and his chums moved in. And it smells like there's a body rotting under the sofa."

"Perhaps there is," I suggested.

"There's isn't. I checked. I refuse to spend the night there."

I was very disappointed about this because I distinctly remember showing Max when he was sixteen how to clean a toilet (many times in fact) to prepare him for the time he had his own place. I'd even taught him how to cook, so you can imagine my frustration when he spent the food money on oven chips and cigarettes.

I wish I'd spared myself the agony and not gone to see his abode. I had to use the backdoor because the front door has so much junk propped up against it that it won't open. To get to the backdoor you have to push your way through the out-of-control bush that blocks the path. It looks as though Max and his housemates have copied the set of *The Young Ones*★ for the interior. I politely declined the offer of a cup of tea. All the mugs and cups that I could see had cigarette ends floating on the moldy remains. And I'm sure I felt the carpet squelch beneath my feet.

On a positive note, the frosty atmosphere between Max and me made Mia very happy indeed. I was absolutely delighted that her end of year college report for her hairdressing course was littered with "excellent." This was a far cry from

★ Hip British sitcom from the eighties that featured four anarchist students who lived like pigs.

the "must do better" and "must not call the teacher a bitch" I'd had to suffer in her school reports.

I was so happy with her that I gave her the ten pounds I had intended to give Max to get himself a halfway decent "do." Mia was beside herself with glee because, she said, this was the first time in her life that she had felt like the favorite and gloated that Max was no longer "The Golden Child" as she's sneeringly called him since she could speak.

Now it was my turn to look up to heaven. "Max wasn't my favorite. I don't have a favorite. I love you both exactly the same," I said wearily.

"You always liked Max more than me."

Max put his fingers in his ears and started making loud noises. Then he got into a fetal position and started sucking his thumb. "Think of a happy place," he cooed, "think of a happy place."

As usual, Max defused the situation by making us laugh.

It wasn't that I liked or loved Max more than Mia but she was born feisty, which can be exhausting and frustrating if you are used to a firstborn who is obedient and easygoing.

They did squabble a lot but there was plenty of fun and laughter. We loved playing basketball and badminton in the garden. Mia was really good at badminton. Still is. I'd have Mia as my badminton partner over Max any day.

I took my responsibility as a parent very seriously and read many books on how to be the best mother I could. I learned you should tell your children the facts of life as soon as they start asking questions about it.

One thing I knew for sure was that I wouldn't say what my mother had told me when I was eleven and already knew anyway: "The man plants his seed in the woman's vagina." Our neighbor was pregnant when Max and Mia were seven and five, so I shouldn't have been too surprised that they would want to know how a baby gets inside a woman's tummy.

I was concentrating on drying them after their bath and before I knew it the words came tumbling out: "The man plants his seed in the woman's vagina."

I don't think I have ever been so full of self-loathing but was pleasantly surprised that they didn't want more details. Finally, Mia requested clarification: "Why would a man want to plant a seed in my pajamas?"

"When a man and a woman are in love, they get married and if they want to have a baby, the man puts his penis, willy, inside the lady's vagina, front bottom, and a seed comes out which may or may not grow into a baby." I hated myself.

Max thought about this for a while then collapsed in a fit of uncontrollable laughter.

"I can't wait to tell Robert Hodder about this at school tomorrow," he said

Mia spent the next couple of years checking her pajamas were seed free before she would put them on.

The car journey up to the Lake District for brother Mark's surprise fortieth birthday party was just like old times with the kids constant bickering, laughing at my expense, and singing at the tops of their voices. "Just messing with your mind, Mum," they kept saying reassuringly.

There's a lot to be said for seeing your children once every three months.

25

Farty Forty

Mark was totally shocked but very happy to see us pull up outside the Old Dungeon Ghyll Hotel in Ambleside that his wife, Lisa, had booked to host a weekend of activities to celebrate the Bro's fortieth. He'd thought that it was just him, Lisa, and their two girls who were going away.

Mum and Dad had already arrived. Mark turned to Mum when he saw Julia and me and said: "I'm sorry, Mother, but I have to say 'fuck' and warn you that there is every chance I am going to drink so much that I will end up naked." Queen Victoria never looked so disapproving.

Julia and Mark used to sing in the same band, The Noble Crooners, until Julia left Hampshire for London to seek her fortune and try and make the big time. Mark and the rest of the band had "responsibilities" and day jobs so didn't want to take the risk.

Because they share the singing gene, Julia is closer to Mark than I am. It must be difficult for him that Julia became the musical talent because Mark was the star singer in the family when they were younger. When Mark was looking round Julia's fabulous new London home, bought with the proceeds of her singing and songwriting he told her: "You are living the life I always dreamed. I should hate you but I don't. I'm very proud of you. I just didn't have the tenacity required to survive the music business."

Mark never recovered from the frustration and bitter disappointment of scraping the money together when he was about twenty to catch a train to London to go for an audition for a band. He had spent hours rehearsing. He stood outside the theatre in the cold and rain for hours with hundreds of other hopefuls when some bastard with a clipboard came out and asked all those who weren't members of the Musicians' Union to raise their hands. Mark raised his, along with many others, who were told they wouldn't be needed.

As Hunter S. Thompson said: "The music business is a cruel and shallow money trench, a long plastic hallway where thieves and pimps run free, and good men die like dogs . . . there is also a negative side."

Mark poured all his artistic talent and energy into The Noble Crooners who still perform locally in Hampshire but minus the girl singer. The original band's reunion is always a great musical event. Dad's seventieth birthday was the last time, now they would be back together for Mark's fortieth.

Mark is very funny, just like our Dad. He never complains. Everything is always "marvelous." He is a devoted father. He drives two and a half hours to work and back every day to provide for his family. He's a salesman for a computer company and has impossible targets to reach every month. He smokes like a chimney, uses loads of butter and cream when he cooks, and is, in my opinion, a heart attack waiting to happen.

Mark and I never really connected like Julia and I, but I remember him as a cheeky, mischievous, hugely appealing, and likeable child who regularly got caned★ at school for smoking behind the bicycle shed. He is the best joke teller I've ever met and a terrific, fun Dad. He is a staunch supporter of the English national cricket, rugby and football squads, and a very useful member of any pub quiz team.

Throughout his birthday, Mark's many friends, including the rest of The Noble Crooners, arrived from all over the country. Mark was drunk by 5 P.M. but managed to stay clothed and was the last to leave the bar at 2:30 A.M. The only other person I think may have drunk as much as him was Max who poured pint after pint of Theakston's Old Peculiar† with Remy Martin chasers down his neck.

Max, Mia, and I were sharing a room and by far the worst consequence of Max's overindulgence was the most pernicious wind in the history of flatulence.

I protested: "It's not funny. The elderly couple in the next room might think it's me making that disgusting noise."

I admit this was madness on my part as it made Max strain even more until his duvet was levitating and Mia and I were hanging out of the window, gasping for air.

The next day at breakfast a steady stream of sorry looking men with hangovers crawled into the dining room. The Inn Keeper had cooked a splendid breakfast, complete with home-made marmalade, which the hungover and abstemious tucked into with equal gusto. Lisa, who is an expert mountain walker had arranged for the fit, keen, and, in my view, slightly mad to go on a seven-mile hike up Bow Fell. I knew my limitations

★ Teacher's favorite method of corporal punishment in our day, which involved thwacking a child's bottom with a cane.

† Strong Northern English real ale that looks and tastes like treacle.

and told the gathered throng that I would do the honorable thing and stay behind to keep Mum and Mia company.

Dad insisted that he was spry and fit enough to cope with the challenge that, historically, has brought men twenty years younger to their knees.

The torrential rains and howling winds arrived at about 3 P.M. When none of the twenty-five in the party had returned by six, I started to worry. Then four weary souls arrived soaked to the skin and shivering with cold. They told us through chattering teeth that Dad had got into difficulty on the way up and instead of turning back as any sensible person would, he insisted on carrying on. The others had been forced to follow Dad's snail's pace and were freezing and exhausted.

Long story short, Dad had to be rescued. The Inn Keeper valiantly drove his four-wheel drive as close to the rest of the party as conditions would allow and drove Dad back to the hotel.

Julia told me later: "Dad would never have made it if he'd had to walk the last two miles under his own steam. I thought he was a goner." Max, apparently, was quite a hero and stayed with Dad the whole time and generally kept everyone's spirits up.

The hike had taken eight tortuous hours, which gave everyone half an hour to get ready for the slap-up dinner and ceilidh.★ Dinner was running late as the Inn Keeper had to interrupt his cooking to rescue Dad.

Dad protested: "I did not need rescuing. I don't know what all the fuss was about. I was perfectly okay after a cup of

★ Highland dance gathering pronounced "kayly" that involves flamboyant dancing and the drinking of copious amounts of alcohol. One of the many Scottish inventions that the English pretend is theirs (ours).

tea and a hot bath." Mum whispered that she'd had to help
Dad in and out of the bath as he could barely move he was so
exhausted and his back had seized up.

Julia was still frozen to the bone five days later. I felt fine
but was dreading the ceilidh part of the evening.

I can't abide all that "Swing Your Partners" nonsense and
told Julia: "Nothing, repeat nothing, is going to get me up
doing the Gay Gordon's.* The only Gordon's I'll be enjoying
tonight will be of the gin variety."

Clearly everyone at the party felt the same as me because
they all buggered off to the bar as soon as the musicians took
up their instruments. Well, you could have knocked me down
with a hair from a horse's tail when I noticed that the man
leading the band on the fiddle was none other than our marmalade making, mountain rescuing, master chef hero, the Inn
Keeper. Was there no end to the man's talents?

Lisa was desperately trying to rally a foursome onto the
dance floor as the band was playing to an empty room. Julia
said: "As you managed to avoid the drama and exertion of the
hike, the least you can do is step into the breach and help out
by swinging a partner." Julia, Max, Mia, Mark, and I took our
places. Grudgingly. And not before I'd taken a very large gulp
of Gordon's.

"If Californians can do tai chi and yoga in front of complete strangers on the beach at the end of our road, you can do
Morris Dancing† in front of family and friends," Julia said. No
one swung their partners more enthusiastically than me and I
really rather enjoyed myself. It's official, I'm middle-aged.

---

* Dance step, not a dance troupe.
† Eccentric English form of country dancing that involves the waving of
handkerchiefs and the wearing of bells on the knees. Question: Why can't
Jewish men be Morris Dancers? Answer: Because you have to be a complete
dick to be a Morris Dancer.

We finally retired to the bar for a nightcap and a singsong at about 3 A.M. Mum left for bed and whispered to me: "Thank God your brother didn't expose himself. I've been worrying about it all weekend."

By the time we'd finished our Beatles and Crosby, Stills, Nash, and Young repertoire, Mark could barely stand. He stumbled toward the door, fumbled for the handle, then hesitated as it dawned that he'd forgotten something important. A speech perhaps, thanking everyone for their gifts and for coming all this way to celebrate his birthday?

He faced the expectant crowd, scratched his head, wobbled a bit and smiled contentedly as would a cat who had licked the cream. He gave a knowing nod, dropped his trousers and raised his arms above his head in triumph.

I said to Julia: "Now I know why Nanny Fordham said when she first saw him after he was born 'My, he's got a fair section!' Nanny Fordham always had a lovely turn of phrase. She once called Dad a "fornicating old cow bag" after he ate some bread and dripping that she was saving for visitors.

There was much head scratching as everyone said good night. That very week at college, Mia had studied "head lice" on her hairdressing course. A thorough examination of some of the children's scalps the next morning revealed several cases of nits among our party.

Mia announced that everyone must be checked and have their hair washed in nit shampoo as a precaution to prevent the spread of the infestation. Mia and Lisa drove to the local chemist and bought their entire supply of nit lotion. The operation was carried out with military precision, using a conveyor belt system.

We "borrowed" twenty-five chairs from the dining room and set them up in orderly rows in Mark and Lisa's bedroom.

Lisa combed the lotion through the hair and Mia washed it out.

As Mia rinsed the foul-smelling lotion out of my hair, I recalled the time my own children first had nits (after the fourth time you don't get so embarrassed), and how mortified I was that I'd had to suggest to my gentleman caller at the time that he ought to use the nit lotion as a precaution just in case they had leapt onto his head. I never heard from him again.

But that wasn't my most embarrassing moment as a single parent trying to maintain a relationship. I remember when Mia was about five and she'd started answering the phone; I'd given her lessons in how to speak politely and clearly. One day the telephone rang and she picked it up before I could get to it. I heard her say clearly and very loudly: "Mummy can't come to the phone because she's having a poo."

That week at school, her teacher asked all the children in class to say a sentence using the word "polite." Mia said: "It's very polite to do your poos in the toilet."

26

The "M" Word

England was cold, gray, and very wet. Everyone looked miserable and the service was terrible.

There were no other customers in sight as I approached the deli counter in Waitrose.* I politely asked the teenage assistant, who was suffering from a severe case of surly cow syndrome, for a quarter of honey glazed ham.

"You have to take a ticket."

"But there's no one else here."

"You have to take a ticket."

I dutifully obeyed, ashamed that I had tried to bypass the rules.

"Thirty-six!" she barked and glared at me. "Yes?"

"A quarter of honey glazed ham, please." She grudgingly wrapped the meat and threw it on the counter.

"Thirty-seven!"

"There's no one here," I pointed out helpfully.

"Thirty-seven!" she shouted and stared at me with Hannibal Lecter eyes.

There must be a new law that says all British supermarkets

---

* Gelsons.

must employ at least one grumpy old man. He was pricing down the smoked salmon as it was perilously close to its sell by date.

"I'll have one of the larger packets, please," I said.

"I haven't finished marking it down yet," he said sneeringly.

"Okay. Well, when you're ready."

"I'm going from left to right so I may be a while." It gave him immense sadistic pleasure to make me wait as long as possible, pausing regularly to inspect his precious pricing gun, which was in perfect working order.

I still needed some ice cream and foolishly thought that the woman who was by the freezer chest might be able to direct me to the Haagen Daz. "Can't you see I'm fridging up?" she snarled, furious that I'd interrupted her.

She looked perplexed as I expressed the hope that she have a nice day.

I called the Writer as soon as I got back to LA. He was clearly waiting for me—hovering over the phone—hoping against hope that I would call. So I called . . . no response from him for the compulsory two days!!!!

Maybe it was time to let the Writer put his sausage in my honey pot. Well, I had to make sure he wasn't hung like a field mouse, didn't I? He's a lousy boyfriend but he might be a great lover. I agreed to spend the weekend at his place. Then, thanks to the most enormous cosmic cock-up, I started my period on Friday. God, why dost thou torment me so?

Assuming that he wasn't such a shallow bastard that my bringing Peter Period along for the sleepover would have him running to the Hollywood Hills, I went anyway. I thought he took the news quite well and I assumed that we'd still enjoy some level of intimacy.

He wore his big baggy tee shirt and even baggier shorts to bed. I, in retaliation, wore my nightdress that I'd packed in case it was cold in the morning. Julia calls it my "stay single" nightie. The Writer's two cats slept between us. Did I mention that he snored? At one point he told me that if I didn't stop fidgeting, he'd smother me with a pillow. Good first night.

And another thing. He cracks his knuckles. Having just read an article entitled "How to Be Assertive and Not Aggressive," I asked him, politely, to refrain from cracking them in my presence as I found it annoying. I followed this up with an inquiry as to what he found irritating, to ensure that I didn't offend him.

Immediately, he retorted: "Farting. I can't stand people farting. There was a guy at work who kept coming into my office and farting. I told him that if he let rip in my office again, I'd jump on his desk, drop my trousers, and shit in his out tray."

Now call me old-fashioned, but I felt this wasn't the most charming conversation that I'd ever entered into with a man. "Would you really have shit in his out tray?" I asked.

"Oh yes," he said, "and he knew it. He never farted in my office again."

Neither did I.

The next night was a girls' night out at the Las Palmas Club in Hollywood where Jeff Goldblum's jazz band was playing. He's a really good piano player. We'd gone because Judith was singing a couple of songs with him. Between numbers, my girlie best mates wanted to know all about my dirty weekend and why it hadn't been dirty.

We were standing in the patio area so Moira could have a smoke. She was appalled that the Writer hadn't been intimate and affectionate. "I mean, after all, there are plenty of other places he could have put his pink torpedo even if he couldn't put it up your ninny nonny noo."

There was a moment's silence before the rest of us asked in unison "Like where?" She sucked heavily on an American Spirit and said, in a tone that was a bit too knowing: "Under your armpit. In between your toes."

Mr. Goldblum starting playing "My Funny Valentine" and Judith went to join him on stage so we were distracted, but I overheard Suzanne whispering to Julia that she never understood why some people were so squeamish about having sex at period time. Julia, who wouldn't even discuss it, looked repulsed.

I had lunch with the Writer two days in a row. He can see me for lunch but not for dinner. Interesting. He sensed my irritation: "I'm pretty sure I'm commitment phobic. Look, I've got a deadline and writing is my priority. This is the first time in recent history that I've seen a woman for two lunches in a row so you should be flattered."

I said: "Snooze and you lose, my friend."

He said: "I hope you'll wear one, in fact several condoms if you're going to shag someone else."

I said: "Funnily enough, I'm more concerned about getting pregnant than catching a sexually transmitted disease."

He said, expressing genuine surprise: "Really? I didn't realize you could still get pregnant."

The bastard thinks I'm menopausal!

27

Muttley No Mates

I have been feeling kind of strange lately, especially during Peter Period, like my head is full of cotton wool. Julia confirmed my suspicion that I have been rather intolerant and impatient of late. After a lengthy silence, I wondered: "Do you think there might be a chance, obviously a remote one, that I might be, possibly, menopausal?"

She gave a kindly and knowing nod like a nurse of many years' experience. "I have been wondering but didn't like to mention it."

I told her to sod off and stormed out in a huff.

I remember years ago writing in the *Dorset Evening Echo* about the benefits of the yam for menopausal women. You could buy a cream and rub it into your inner elbow then sail through the big "M." No hot flushes. Nothing. It costs $25 these days!

A lady in Wild Oats recommended "Estrotone" at $20 a throw. I said: "I think I'll try and pull myself together before I splash out that kind of money. I'm already spending $100 a month on supplements to keep me young and healthy. It would be cheaper to have a face-lift."

Stem cell replacement therapy is all the rage here but it

costs $25,000 a pop and you can only get it in the Bahamas. And then there's the dead fetus dilemma attached to it, which is even more repugnant a concept than Hormone Replacement Therapy being largely pregnant horse's pee.

What with the onslaught of the menopause shock and my gentleman caller dilemma, I decided I needed some quiet time for reflection so I took Muttley to the dog park. Nobody wants to play with him either. When the others dogs bark at him because they don't want him in their gang, he cowers under my seat. He really is a bit of a wimp. I told him: "Bugger off and play and let me read my book in peace."

Julia was invited by Judith to go to a recording of the *Tonight Show* as Spinal Tap was performing and she was singing backing vocals for them. It wasn't a Plus One invitation as the tickets were like gold dust, so I couldn't tag along with Julia.

She could see how disappointed I was (I used a look I've seen Muttley use to great effect when he wants something) and said I could go in her place. Julia said: "Are you sure about this? I'm not confident you'll make it to Burbank on your own. It's a bit of a trek and you always get lost on the 101."

We studied a map for three hours, turning it every which way. I said: "I can do this."

"Well, if you are sure," she said unconvinced.

Easy mistake, I went north instead of south on the 101 and ended up in Topanga Canyon. I don't know how, either. I finally managed to get through to Spinal Tap's dressing room on the cellular phone. Derek Smalls, the bass guitarist, kindly talked me through the journey until I was safely in the NBC lot. I just made it into my seat in time.

One of the other guests was the NBC sports presenter, Bob Costas, who Jay Leno had been ribbing on a previous show for dyeing his hair, something Bob strenuously denied live on air during NBC's Olympic coverage. As if the nation could care less. He offered to donate a lock of hair to be scientifically analyzed for any traces of Grecian 2000 or similar colorant.

He then turned to the audience and asked if anyone believed the crazy notion that his hair might be dyed. I was the only one who put my hand up and had to suffer the consequences. The best riposte he could come up with was: "You are clearly insane, madam." He doth protest too much.

Judith and Derek Smalls suggested I follow their limousine home to make sure I didn't get lost as they only live around the corner from us. They said they'd get their driver to pull in and wait for me to catch up in the Mustang.

Long story short, every guest on the show had their own limo. I followed the wrong one and ended up in Beverly Hills. Julia had to talk me home on the cell phone as she traced my progress on the map. The "L" for loser sign soon started to wear very thin. Now Julia has a new one for me, which is causing her the utmost amusement. It's three downward pointing fingers on the forehead as in "M" for menopausal. Fairly amusing if it is at someone else's expense.

She wasn't so amused when Muttley had a run in with the law because she had him off his leash on the grassy knoll at the end of our road. She thought she'd get away with it as they were under cover of darkness. I wasn't there to witness their fear and shame as I was busy making Julia's birthday cake.

Apparently the cop, complete with truncheon and hand on holster, came over to the felons and shone his torch in

Muttley's eyes before checking his identity tag. The poor hound was petrified.

I said to Julia: "Lucky for you I queued for two hours to get Muttley his license otherwise the pair of you would have been banged to rights★ and hit in the pocket with a hefty fine. Who'd have been a loser then, eh?"

★ Slang for getting thrown in jail.

28

Deal Breakers

Max has taken a part-time job at an art college until Side Salad Records starts making a profit. He told me: "I've been formally reprimanded at work for writing poetry during office hours. What nobler reason could there possibly be for getting sacked than writing poetry?"

"Using the company phone to make a fortune on the stock market? Did you buy some decent shoes with the money I sent you?"

"No, Mother, I did not."

"Why not?"

"Because I have made two pledges to myself. One is to never have a mobile phone, the other is to never wear sensible shoes."

"Are you still smoking?"

"Yes, I am."

I can't believe or bear it that both my children smoke like chimneys. I tried leaving photographs of cancerous lungs around the house and quotes from the many articles I cut out on the subject, like how much money they'll have burned up in smoke during their lifetime if they keep up their current pack-a-day habit (a hundred thousand pounds. Each!) and that smoking will probably kill them, but to no avail.

Christine the Doctor told me once: "I made a decision very early on in my medical training that I'd never marry a smoker as it's a given that you'll spend the last twenty years of your married life taking care of them when they are sick with cancer or heart disease."

I'll choose my moment carefully, but I think I'll drop that bit of useful info into the conversation next time I see them. Julia says the main reason they smoke is because I don't want them to.

I said huffily: "Six months experience as a dog owner and suddenly you're an expert on parenting."

Apart from the health issue, I am worried that Max and Mia will be treated like social outcasts by everyone except Moira in California. Smokers are not welcome here, either in peoples' homes or public places. It's against the law to smoke, except in the privacy of your own home. I've noticed the other neighbors frowning upon the two ashtrays on the porch that are always filled to overflowing with dog ends when the children are visiting.

Which brings me to the subject of deal breakers in a relationship. While I am put off by smokers and knuckle crackers, Julia hasn't noticed that her gentleman caller is an inveterate cracker of his finger joints. He slowly pulls each individual digit until it pops then interlocks his fingers and cracks the entire bunch. Sometimes he cracks his neck from side to side.

He carefully places his hands on his ears then snaps his head to the left and right. He has to do it carefully as he broke his neck once in a skiing accident. He's very accident-prone and has broken every bone in his body, including his back. A collision with a UPS truck that mounted the pavement as he was waiting to cross the road was his most spectacular accident. The brain surgery left him without a sense of smell.

I don't think he realizes how influential I am in Julia's life and that the sooner he cracks the irritating habit instead of his fingers and neck the more chance he has of enjoying a long and fruitful association with my kid sister. I've already mentioned that I find it offensive but it seems to have slipped his mind.

Suzanne told me over cocktails in the Casa Del Mar that she hasn't had a proper boyfriend in seven years.

"What was your last boyfriend like?" I asked.

"He was fantastic. Kind, loving, handsome, had a great job, and wanted to marry me," she said.

I asked, perplexed: "What went wrong?"

"He played air drums."

"Do you think you might have been a little hasty in chucking this ideal man for something so minor?"

"Not at all," she said. "For me, playing air drums is a deal breaker."

Mum told me that her mother declined a marriage proposal because her suitor crunched a Polo mint[*] when he took her on a date to the pictures.[†] Now I can fully understand that and this worries me as being forty-something does kind of narrow the field, as it were. I might add that the man who might have been my step-grandfather was a man with a good job and my grandmother was an impoverished widow with nine children and not, one might be forgiven for thinking, a woman who could afford to be quite so picky.

I thought things might be looking up on the job front but lunch with the TV Producer, who's married to Christine the

[*] A mint with a hole.
[†] Movies.

Doctor, didn't go as well as I'd hoped. He said: "I'm working on a new TV program that might suit you. I know you are capable of presenting the show but, frankly, you are too old. You could be an assistant producer on it, if you like."

I said: "That's nice."

29

Unlucky for Some

Now, while I knew the Writer wasn't "the one" for me, I wouldn't have been the least bit offended if he'd felt I was "the one" for him.

We played phone tag for a week. Then he left this message: "Look, I don't think this is going to work. I've got to go back to Scotland to work on a TV program. Friendship is always the most enduring path, so let's have lunch when I get back."

I stared at the answer phone. "That's nice."

I console myself that he was always half an hour late for dinner, always working to a deadline, and the last time we went to the movies he leant across, pointed the straw of his fizzy drink toward me, and asked with a filthy twinkle in his eye: "Do you want to suck my Coke?"

Much worse, and without any consultation, Julia's gentleman caller has suddenly been promoted to "Boyfriend."

They're spending so much time together that most of my evenings are now spent dog sitting. Which is how I came to be lying on the sofa with Muttley in my arms, gazing into my face with rapt attention.

"Who'd have thought it would come to this? You're the

only male in the United States of America who cares a flying fig about me." Which is probably why I'm channel hopping in the faint hope of catching a glimpse of Jennifer and Brad's nuptials. Go girl!

I explained to Muttley that according to Moira: "Brad and Jen's marriage is definitely going to last because not only are their sun signs super compatible, they have the added astrological bonus of Jen's Sagittarius moon being in Brad's Sagittarius sun and vice versa—his Aquarius moon in her Aquarius sun. This makes them true soul mates, apparently. Well, dippy bloody do for them."

Now the TV Producer thinks I'm too old to appear on his TV program and must be kept behind the scenes for fear of repulsing his viewers. "Well, I tell you what, Muttley, he's dead wrong. Oh my God, I'm talking to a dog."

I continued: "The idea for the show is that the five female presenters live together in a fabulous house from where they broadcast live a daily hour-long magazine program. *The Real World* meets *The View* meets *Friends* meets *Sex and the City.*

"Bearing in mind the daytime TV audience is largely stay-at-home mums, they don't want to watch twenty-four-year-old mouthy, skinny babes who know diddly squat about life and family. They want a woman of the world who's had kids, been broke and lonely, wants to be loved and cherished by a good man and, like them, thinks she needs to lose at least seven pounds—a proper experienced journalist who can interview celebrities and politicians alike by cutting out the sycophantic bull shit. Someone like me who's, ahem, thirty-five." Muttley appeared to nod his head in agreement.

Julia's birthday party the following evening was a huge success with everyone telling me how fabulous, gorgeous, and what a great cook I am. Grown men wept at the sight and taste of the birthday cake. I said to Julia: "If I'm so bloody wonderful, how come I haven't got a boyfriend?"

The Birthday Girl did well on the gift front: seven copies of *Joni Mitchell: The Complete Poems and Lyrics,* twelve fancy candles, and a book on homo-erotic art. She received a very nice handbag as well, which Muttley much preferred to the birthday cake. Or perhaps he had a fit of jealousy because she was the center of attention. I still don't fully understand his Fijian ways. He also ate a boogie board this week, which wasn't ours to eat.

The morning after the party, I found the Boyfriend making himself an omelet in MY kitchen. He's becoming quite the regular fixture around here.

Julia declined the opportunity to have a girls' night out with Moira, Suzanne, and me. She said: "No, thanks. You go without me. It'll be a chance for Boyfriend and me to have the house to ourselves for a change. We'll be able to play naked Scrabble."

30

And the Emmy Goes to . . .

Moira has found a lump in her right breast, just below her armpit. An ultrasound revealed a 3.2 centimeter lump. Not only was the lump cancerous, the cancer has spread to nine lymph nodes and she doesn't have medical insurance.

Being the resourceful Aquarian that she is, Moira managed to get herself included in a breast cancer program that helps fund the frighteningly expensive treatment for three "lucky" women a year.

The surgeon has recommended a six-month course of chemotherapy, which will bring on an early menopause, which means she won't be able to have children. Now she's awaiting the results of a body scan to see if the cancer has spread to any other parts of her body. If it has, she is royally buggered. She declined the mastectomy option and is just having the lump removed followed by the chemo and radiation.

Inspired by Moira's determination to beat her challenge, I called the TV Producer and told him that I think he may have been a little hasty in saying I'm too old to be one of the presenters of *Room Mates* and why.

After a three second pause that felt like three weeks he said: "You're absolutely right. I'll call you back."

And he did call back to say that he wanted to shoot a pilot the very next day and did I know someone who could be the "slutty" one. Suzanne does a stand-up comedy routine that is bloody funny and extremely slutty. I particularly like her Barbara Stanwyck impression.

Suzanne and I turned up at an amazing house in Malibu, she nursing a broken heart having been dumped by some bloke she'd been dating for two weeks and me with a severe headache that was probably brought on because Julia had told me that morning that she felt repulsed when she watched me brush my teeth, so would I mind waiting until she'd finished using the facilities before I invaded her bathroom space? Ever the professionals, Suzanne and I painted on our smiles and waited for "action."

There were three other "room mates." Another comedienne who is very good at crafts, a twice-divorced twenty-eight-year-old mother of a two-year-old daughter, and another actress who's a great cook.

We spent the day in different parts of the house talking about issues of the day but mostly knob sizes, lousy lovers we have known, and the trouble with men generally, while learning how to make coconut fried chicken and decorate a jewel-encrusted paving stone.

Things got a bit nasty after I mentioned My George about three times, quite humorously actually, and the stand-up comedienne (the one who isn't my friend) said: "For God's sake stop droning on about George Clooney. You sound like a broken record. Mel Brooks is a more likely conquest for you, anyway."

This from a woman who is happy for the world to know

that she likes fat men who sweat a lot during sex, most no-
tably the big cop in *Third Watch*. She said: "I love it when
their potbelly rubs up and down on my clitoris and makes me
orgasm." I nearly choked on a wishbone and just stopped myself from turning *Room Mates* into a women's wrestling tour-
nament.

I was quite pleased with the interview I did with Suzanne
(brag) about the film she was in with Madonna, *The Next
Best Thing,* or the "Next Worst Thing" as I called it. She
agreed that the reason the film wasn't a success is because the
script sucked and Madonna is a singer, not an actress.

She didn't mince words about Jim Carrey either, having
just finished filming with him. "Not only is Jim weird," she
said, "he's not particularly nice."

I know enough about this business we call show that
these programs can take forever to get picked up, if at all, so
I'm not holding my breath. Even if the studio bosses like the
idea, they might not like me. Luckily for my self-esteem, I'm
very good at coping with rejection.

I remember a writer friend (not THE Writer) telling me
how he stuck his rejection letters on his bedroom wall having
vowed that he'd kill all the people who'd rejected him for
jobs one by one if it ever came to pass that there was no room
left to put up the last one.

There are 173 men and women in England who should
count themselves lucky that he finally got a job, at the BBC,
as a script reader. This was in the days when the BBC had a
script development unit. He told me that they used to receive
thirteen thousand unsolicited manuscripts a year, of which
one might get made into a television program.

I've been thinking about earning some serious money by
writing a movie but it's almost impossible to get one made.

Last year, some thirty-seven-thousand screenplays were registered with the Writer's Guild of America. Only two hundred were made into films. That's encouraging, isn't it?

Julia and I were having lunch with Moira and her sister, Naomi, at Babaloo on Montana when the call came through from the hospital to say that Moira's cancer hasn't spread. We laughed and we cried and we hugged, oblivious to the stares of the other customers.

Meanwhile, Moira has given up alcohol and smoking. Canadian researchers have found that women who began smoking within five years of starting their periods are around 70 percent more likely to develop cancer later in life and it really messes with your immune system, so it's harder to fight the cancer cells if they turn up elsewhere in the body.

We've all become experts on the subject. The main causes of breast cancer are thought to be alcohol, a high fat diet, lack of exercise, and a family history. One book I read said cancer is 41 percent lifestyle, 29 percent genetic, and 30 percent bad luck. I've cut down my own alcohol intake. Instead of having a couple of glasses of Merlot five or six times a week, I'm only going to drink two or three nights a week and absolutely no drinking at lunchtime. There's a theory that California wines should be avoided as a number of wine growers here add too many sulphites to their plonk. I now only drink French red wine. Although Danny at Surf Liquor insists that all wines, including French, have to have sulphites to stop them from going bad.

Naomi has read that the dramatic increase in the number of cases of breast cancer may be attributable to the extensive use of deodorants, so Julia and I are trying an organic one. We've already changed to bleach-free tampons and stopped drinking diet drinks because of the aspartame, which can also give you cancer.

In her book *The Cure for All Cancers,* Hulda Regehr Clark claims that all patients with cancer have high levels of iso-propyl alcohol and flook worms in their body. Get rid of the parasite and the isopropyl alcohol in the body and the cancer will go, she says.

She also reckons that because pet food is heavily polluted with aflatoxins and solvents, including benzene, pets also get the human intestinal flook, which are plentiful in saliva, so she says, "Never kiss your pet." Even though I would be dev-astated if Julia was sick, the irony would not be lost on me if she caught cancer from Muttley. She's always kissing him.

31

Fantasy Boyfriends

Max and Mia are here for their summer holiday, which is fantastic apart from the fact that Mia keeps asking me deeply personal questions like how many men have you slept with? Julia thinks it's all healthy and marvelous and indicates that Mia wants to have a truly authentic relationship with me.

While Max was taking his cousin, Muttley, to the dog park, the three girls were sitting in the garden drinking tea and eating cake when Mia asked me: "Have you got a fantasy boyfriend?" In the spirit of honesty and authenticity, I said: "George Clooney."

"That's amazing. He's mine as well."

Julia collapsed in fits of uncontrollable laughter. I was aghast.

"You might think it's amazing but I think it's perverted that my daughter, my own flesh and blood, and I fantasize about the same man." I pulled rank and told her she must find herself a new fantasy boyfriend.

She thought about it for a moment: "Robert Downey Jr. was released from prison this week so I'll have him as my Fantasy Boyfriend."

I decided it was time for me to find a Reserve Fantasy

Boyfriend. I didn't have long to wait. The next night we went to see Sting play at the Greek Theatre. The man is gorgeous and, incredibly, more than fifty years old. All that yoga and tantric sex clearly agrees with him. I leant toward Julia during "Message in a Bottle": "I think I've found my reserve fantasy boyfriend."

She got quite high and mighty. "Sting," she said, "has been my Fantasy Boyfriend since 1984 and I'm not prepared to share him with anyone, least of all you."

I said: "You've already got a boyfriend."

She shrieked (she had to shout as Sting was playing "Roxanne" very loudly): "He is my Actual Boyfriend not my Fantasy Boyfriend. They're not the same thing."

The people behind us asked us to shut up and then Robert Downy Jr. came on to sing a duet with Julia's "Fantasy Boyfriend." It was difficult to see who it was at first, many in the audience thought it was Julio Iglesias's boy but I knew immediately that it was Downey as I'm very good at celebrity spotting.

Mia nearly fainted with shock: "I never dreamed I'd see him in real life." Well, obviously she had dreamed of it but the whole point of fantasy is that it never actually happens in reality because then it's not technically or even literally a fantasy anymore.

I told Mia he'd probably be at the after-show party as well, so she might get to meet him. She suppressed a sob: "He's been through so much. I want to marry him and take care of him."

"Over my dead body. A gun carrying, alcoholic, drug addict is not what I had in mind for my son-in-law," I muttered.

Julia had been invited to the after-show party by Sting's keyboard player and the producer of *Brand New Day,* Kipper, who Julia has known for years. She managed to get a "plus three." Kipper told me he'd spent so many years in the music business not getting his phone calls returned that he decided to change his name to something that wasn't easily forgotten.

Robert Downey Jr. WAS at the after-show party. Mia didn't actually talk to him as she was too nervous but she did brush past him, several times actually, so she could say in all honesty to anyone who would listen that they had had physical contact.

Julia introduced me to Sting and the lovely Mrs. Sting. I managed to stutter a hello before stumbling from my too high heels and spilling my glass of Dom Perignon perilously close to Sting's Versace jacket. He wasn't fazed at all. He must be used to ordinary mortals making complete fools of themselves in his presence.

His wife, Trudi, is just as cool. I think she was wearing Armani. So was I. The only difference being that my Armani jacket is six years old and one of Julia's castoffs.

Mia, Julia, and I danced with Sting! Not naked or anything but on the dance floor at the 360 Club. There were a hundred other people on the dance floor as well but so what. Max had gone off to an area "where there aren't so many pheromones."

I liked the way Sting was with his children. I saw his teenage son embrace him and tell his dad that his show had been great that night. It was. Sting smiled proudly, ruffled his son's hair, and told him to tie up his shoelaces before he tripped over them. At the end of the day, he's still a parent. I've always been strict about shoelaces being tied as well.

Even though Sting is clearly gorgeous and amazing, he's a workaholic and has been on the road promoting *Brand New Day*, doing six shows a week for eighteen straight months. Once this world tour is finished, he's going straight back to the studio to start recording his next album. I'd soon get bored of the rock 'n' roll lifestyle staying night after night in a different Four Seasons hotel, the limos, the designer clothes. Chance would be a fine thing.

But if Julia is going to have a "Fantasy Boyfriend" who she's actually met, I'm going to have David Do-Shag-Me as Reserve Fantasy Boyfriend. We were finally introduced at a party at the Hollywood Manager's house the following week. He's nothing like his Fox Mulder character in *X-Files* who never smiles. He's charming, witty and very handsome, and he was sporting a 5-o'clock shadow that's always been a blatant turn on for me.

He joined our group just as we were discussing how many people we'd not slept with who we wish we had and how many we'd slept with who we wish we hadn't. I could only think of one man I've slept with I wish I hadn't and two I didn't at the time but wish I had.

Dave (his friends call him Dave) said: "I've never regretted sleeping with anyone but there are many women I haven't slept with but wish I had." Then he took my hand as if to lead me off to the bedroom. The implication being that he was prepared to put his one-eyed trouser snake in MY love canal. I didn't think it was that funny a concept but everyone else thought it hilarious.

32

Unlucky Break

I received a call from ITN last week asking me to do a phone interview on Madonna's new baby for the *Early Morning News*. It was one of those unfortunate stories when absolutely no information is available save for the fact that she had said on KISS FM radio the week before that she didn't want to have her baby in England where she now lives as English hospitals are so Victorian. She felt it best to have her baby in Los Angeles in case anything went wrong.

It's true, Madonna, the gaslight in British hospitals is supposed to be very bad for baby. But something did go wrong with the birth and Madonna started hemorrhaging. I wasn't privy to that information at the time so my phone report was pretty useless, but I think I got away with it as I used my posh voice that sounds convincing yet tells the listener absolutely nothing whatsoever.

American healthcare isn't as great as it's cracked up to be either. There are horror stories here too—like what happened to Julia's boyfriend in Santa Monica.

He was cycling along the bike path with a friend when the friend crashed after he hit a pothole then Boyfriend crashed into him. The friend had a severely gashed leg (blood everywhere), and Boyfriend had a smashed elbow, knee injury, cuts, and bruises.

He was taken to the emergency room on Wilshire and 16th where he waited a couple of hours to get looked at. He was eventually told that he needed emergency surgery on his elbow. They paged the orthopedic surgeon who decided the operation could wait until Tuesday. Could it possibly have been delayed because it was Labor Day weekend, one of the few American bank holidays, and the surgeon had plans?

Knowing how insurance companies can be very particular here, Boyfriend called his, which happens to be in New York where he used to live. Just as he suspected, his policy covers him for emergency treatment and emergency operations anywhere in America but if the surgeon thought it could wait until Tuesday then it couldn't be an emergency so he had to fly to New York for the operation, even though he was in excruciating pain and another doctor at the hospital said that he thought he should be operated on immediately.

After spending eight hours in the ER, a nice doctor eventually gave him a morphine shot and had the decency to look embarrassed as they sent him on his way.

If he had had the expensive operation in Santa Monica on Tuesday, Boyfriend would have had to pay for it himself so the poor man flew to New York in agony with his arm in a temporary cast. He had to pay the $2,250 cost of the flight himself. It was so expensive because it was a holiday weekend. Boyfriend's chum wasn't insured at all and is not looking forward to receiving the invoice as he is an impoverished student and not a multimillionaire pop singer. God Bless the National Health Service of the United Kingdom!

Julia is beside herself as I still haven't got medical insurance here. I did send away for the form but it's more like a book to fill in so I've been putting it off. Julia won't let me leave the house for fear I'll get hit by a car.

On a happier note, the kids have been having the time of their lives here. We went to a script read through of *The Simpsons*. There have been parties, dinners, stand-up comedy nights, boogie boarding, shopping, lunching. All in all it was an excellent mother/kids bonding trip.

They are in Aunt Julia's good books as well, as they were so friendly to cousin Muttley and applauded when he "sat" when Julia told him to. He can also lie down when instructed.

I said: "Why don't you teach him to do something useful like putting the plates in the dishwasher?"

Just to get things in perspective, I made Julia watch as Max and Mia did the same tricks as Muttley AND made a cup of tea and a sandwich for me. I rewarded them with a piece of biscuit. I thought it was a nice touch when they panted and woofed. Julia grudgingly applauded then sloped off looking all hurt, but I think I illustrated the point rather well.

I took the kids to see Julia perform at Largo. I said: "Isn't it great that we can go to clubs together now that you are grown-ups."

"In which case," said Max, "could you please stop calling us kids?"

"I'll try. But I can't promise," I said.

I was surprised when Mia asked for a straw in her glass of Coke.

"Aren't you a bit old for straws?"

Mia said: "The idea is to draw attention to one's kissable lips when sucking, thereby increasing one's chances of attracting a mate."

"Interesting," I said.

I remember her refusing to wear dresses at the age of three or to have her hair cut when she was five on the grounds that she didn't tell me what to wear or when to have my hair cut, so why should I tell her. This was a teenager who would not be told what to do by me, or anyone in authority, especially police officers and teachers.

Mia's motto was "there are no rules." She drinks too much, in my opinion, and smokes way too much pot. Never in front of me but I could tell when she did. Short of locking her up, I didn't know how to stop her. Because I haven't tried any drugs, Mia thinks I don't know what I'm talking about. I know for sure marijuana affects some people much more than others. It can make you paranoid, mean, moody, depressed, and difficult to live with and for people like Mia who don't do anything in moderation, it is poison.

I wish I could recall some amusing anecdotes about Mia's teenage years but we were at battle stations most of the time. Max was no help at all. He said that Mia and I were both to blame. Their dad said the problem was that Mia is just like me. Hello? Have I ever been arrested for cannabis possession and had my fingerprints taken at one of Her Majesty's police stations? I don't think so. At least she didn't get charged. "That," said Mia as I drove her home on what was one of the worst nights of my life, "is because it isn't a big deal."

I look at Mia now and see a unique, amazing, independent, determined, sparkling, funny, beautiful, intelligent, incredible young woman but there were times when I was sure that at least one of us wouldn't live long enough to see her reach eighteen.

33

There's an Icon in Our Garden

Max and Mia were smoking on the stoop—the ideal opportunity to quote from an article I'd found on the Internet. "Would you believe it," I said, "lung cancer has overtaken breast cancer as the biggest killer of women in the UK. It says here that cigarettes are potentially death in a packet. Good Lord. Nine out of ten cases of lung cancer are due to smoking. It says."

Mia looked up: "Gee Mum. You tell the best stories." Max puffed repeatedly on his cigarette and told me that statistics didn't apply to him. I said: "That's what Moira used to say. Her hair started falling out yesterday."

Mia looked up to heaven: "For fuck's sake."

Time for my burning martyr voice: "I just want you both to know that when you've died a long and painful death from lung cancer or heart disease, I will take care of your children when you're gone."

That seemed to do the trick. They looked at each other nervously and stubbed the evil weed out. I think I may finally be getting through. Excellent.

Then I picked up one of Muttley's water sprays and squirted Mia: "Watch your language," I said. Instead of cowering in fear and begging forgiveness, Mia picked up another spray and squirted me back. Julia and Max joined in and it soon became a free for all, which I eventually lost. I thought I'd won after I caught them unawares with a bucket of water but I was powerless against the garden hose. Muttley looked at us as if we were raving mad.

Exhausted and soaked I said: "Come on, we've got to get ready for your farewell party tonight." There's only one shower in our little house so it takes a while for everyone to get ready.

Julia has been very patient with the kids around. Mia sleeps with me and Max sleeps on the sofa bed at the front of the house. They do take up an awful lot of space but I guess it's the least she can do as I've been so tolerant of her dog.

Later, while I was preparing the cheese board for our party, Max and Mia came up and started hacking away at the Farmhouse Cheddar. I tapped them on the back of their hands with a wooden spoon and said: "Look, now I'm not earning a regular income, money's very tight and I'm going to have to let one of you go." They looked crestfallen.

"Ha! Just messing with your mind!" I said.

Relieved, Max whipped out a CD from his pocket: "Fear not, Mother Dearest, our financial woes are over. I now have a proper, functioning record company of my own and I want you to have the first advance copy of my record company's first release." I raced over to the CD player, inserted the disc, pressed play and started to cry. Mostly with pride. Track 4 is a catchy little number charmingly titled "Shit the Bed" by a band called Wurzel Miyagi. I thought: "My parents must never hear this."

I said: "I'm so proud of you. This is a huge achievement. I knew you could do it. Well done."

Mia said indignantly: "I'm so sorry to interrupt your precious bonding moment but I would like to know, Mother, if you were moved to tears when I told you that my lecturer had proclaimed my first graduated bob quite the most perfect she had ever seen?"

"I don't think I cried but I distinctly remember feeling very proud," I said after too long a pause.

"But you don't really think I'm very good at hairdressing do you?"

"I most certainly do."

"How come you won't let me cut or color your hair? You don't trust me, do you?"

"I most certainly do."

"Then let me do your hair and makeup for tonight's party."

I knew that I had to answer quickly. Any hesitation would confirm her theory that I think more of her brother and his accomplishments than I do hers.

"I'd love you to do my hair and makeup for the party. Thank you."

"I can do what I like?"

I managed to say: "I trust you implicitly," but I was thinking: "Are you out of your fucking mind?"

Later, as I was putting the finishing touches to the buffet, I overheard Julia say on the phone: "Of course, she'd be very welcome to come but she'll have to smoke outside with all the other smokers." I watched as Julia slowly put the phone down, took a sharp intake of breath and looked at me, ashen. It was awhile before she was able to speak. Finally, she whispered: "Joni Mitchell is coming to our party." Max and I gasped. Mia said: "Who's Joni Mitchell?"

Record producer Larry Klein, who has agreed to produce Julia's next record, used to be married to Joni Mitchell and had called to ask if he could bring his former wife with whom he continues to collaborate musically and is still great friends as his Plus One.

Julia said nervously: "We won't tell anyone that Joni is coming in case she doesn't turn up and then we'll look stupid. And people will keep staring at the door waiting for her to enter."

"Very wise," I said.

Few musicians achieve icon status: Jimi Hendrix if he were still alive, Bob Dylan, any Beatle or Rolling Stone obviously, Sting, Eric Clapton, David Bowie, Prince, Stevie Wonder, Michael Jackson and Madonna I suppose, and then there's Joni Mitchell. She is the Queen of singer-songwriters—the benchmark by which all others are measured and usually found wanting and she's coming to our fucking house!

You don't have to give any warning that an icon is in the vicinity because something happens to the atmosphere when one is near. There is an electrical charge that permeates the room just before they enter. The door opens in slow motion and it's as if the doorway is surrounded in a magical light. Smoke appears and the icon glides through. There is an audible gasp and the gathered throng respectfully splits in two to allow them to walk through.

Ours was dressed in black from head to toe with a matching beret, perched just so; below it cascaded her trademark long, straight blond hair. She carried her Jack Russell, Coco, in one hand and an unlit cigarette in the other: "Has anyone got a light?" she asked.

Julia and I each grab an ashtray and walk forward to present them to her and lead her to the most comfy chair. I was just about to curtsey when Mia burst through and grabbed the Icon by the arm. She had found a kindred spirit: "You can't smoke in here love. Come outside with me." Julia and I were just about ready to faint with embarrassment but the Icon laughed and went off to the garden arm in arm with Mia from where they held court. Pretty soon all the guests were chain-smoking in the garden with the Icon.

Even Moira was smoking. I looked at her in disbelief. "Don't worry. I'm not inhaling." She was wearing a scarf to cover her thinning hair. The chemotherapy is also making her tired and nauseous.

Five ashtrays were filled to overflowing as Mia asked the Icon, who she still didn't know was an icon: "So what do you do, Jone?" (Joni's friends call her Jone.)

"I'm a musician."

"Oh, I love music. I think Madonna is great. The way she reinvents herself musically with each record."

The Icon scoffed: "So she dyes her hair a different color with every record, big fucking deal."

"Fair point, well made, Jone. Cigarette?"

Soon, Max was chatting to the Icon about his record label and telling her jokes at which she laughed heartily. I swear they were flirting with each other. The Icon said to me as she held out her glass for a refill: "I love your children."

"I love them too," I said proudly.

"And I love your hair. So Bohemian!" The Icon was being polite.

I looked absurd. Mia had re-created "Winter," her winning entry for Best Hair and Makeup in her college's end of term competition. Madame de Pompadour meets Mrs. Munster just about sums it up.

"You promise me it's a vegetable dye?" I said.

"Promise. You're lucky I didn't do Autumn, which is all ferns and acorns," she said.

I said: "I find it hard to believe ferns and acorns could

possibly look more ridiculous than twigs, pine cones, and fake snow."

"Ridiculous?"

"Amazing." I think I'm finally getting the hang of parent psychology.

The Icon was the last to leave the party at 2:45 A.M. Muttley had spent the entire night playing with the Icon's dog. Muttley had fallen in love with Coco at first sight and the feeling was clearly mutual, but I had to explain to him that they come from two different worlds and they can never be together. He looked crestfallen.

As we emptied the ashtrays, Julia said: "I used to dream when I was a teenaged, budding singer-songwriter living on Hayling Island that I would one day meet the greatest female singer-songwriter of all time, but I never imagined she'd be sitting in my own home telling me she liked my songs."

As I drove Max and Mia to the airport the next day we sang to the tune of "There's a Hole in My Bucket": "There's an Icon in Our Garden, Dear Mummy, Dear Mummy . . ."

"The ash tray is fuuuullll, dear mummy, dear mummy . . ."

"Then empty it, dear children, dear children . . ."

34

Desperately Seeking Someone

The Furniture Shop Lady on Main Street had kindly invited Julia (Plus One) to a party at her store, Ashland & Hill. Nine P.M. sharp. We couldn't understand why all the men were wearing white linen suits and sunglasses, and the women looked like Madonna in *Desperately Seeking Susan*.

A lady who claimed to be a clairvoyant told us that the party had a theme—*Miami Vice*—but not before she told me how great my costume was. I said to Julia: "I have to buy myself some new clothes before I become a sartorial joke in this town."

Only last week a sales assistant in Betsey Johnson on Main Street told Julia she looked fabulous as we walked in. She clearly felt obliged to say something to me as well so she looked me up and down and said after a long pause: "And you look very comfortable."

But I digress, the Clairvoyant said: "I wanted to meet you two as you look interesting."

I said: "You think we're lesbians, don't you?"

"Aren't you?"

"No. Sisters."

"You should both come to one of my clairvoyant master

classes and learn how to tap into the power that's within us all," and handed us her card.

I whispered to Julia: "She can't be a very good clairvoyant if she thinks we're gay!"

It was an amazing party. Lots of bright young things and some grown-ups like us. Julia, our new best friend the Clairvoyant, and I were busy checking out the other guests as she told us that she'd left her first husband after eighteen years (no children), then spent two years clearing out her aura before she met her present husband to whom she's been happily married for two months.

She told the cosmos when she was ready for love and the cosmos provided as the cosmos always does.

"How marvelous," I said.

I thought: "What utter bollocks."

I raised my arms to the heavens: "Oh, mighty cosmos, please send me a handsome, loving boyfriend who's rich."

The next night at Julia's Largo gig, a man came up to me, shook me warmly by the hand and told me that I don't know him but he knows me because he's seen the *Room Mates* pilot. Ten times!

He's the agent of the TV Producer. He said: "The program idea is a great one, the pilot is terrific, and you are fantastic in it. It's a tragedy all the major TV studios passed on it."

"Thanks for letting me know," I said.

Julia could see my look of disappointment. "Come on. Let's go home and have a nice cup of tea," she said.

Moira continues to be chipper despite her cancer ordeal. Judith has bought her a fantastic, custom-made wig as Moira has now lost all her hair. Suzanne is organizing a hat shower. We each take a fabulous hat for her so she'll have a magnificent collection to choose from. Our dear, brave friend had already cut her beautiful, long hair short so it wouldn't come as such a devastating blow when it fell out, but nothing prepares you for the shock of seeing your bald pate in the mirror for the first time.

She said stoically: "I've read on the Internet that people who have lots of friends have a better chance of surviving cancer, which is why I really believe I can beat this."

Julia and I have reverted to proper deodorant. Calendula Blossom might not give you breast cancer, but we stank so badly after our morning jog along the beach that we've decided to take our chances with Right Guard.

35

Just the Job

I've finally filled in the form for my medical insurance. Despite many discussions with an insurance broker, who was extremely patient with me, I am still none the wiser about the difference between an HMO and a PPO but have decided to opt for PPO with a $2,000 deductible because that's what Julia's got.

I now know why 41 million Americans don't have health insurance. It's because they can't afford it. $152 a month! Julia's is less than $100 a month because she's under forty. I've spoken to some people who pay up to $400 dollars a month.

Each time we go to our GP we have to cough up $45 for the doctor as a co-payment and then any drugs, tests, and treatment are on top of that and if we have a major accident we still have to pay the first $2,000. Does that seem fair?

Meanwhile, Boyfriend is making steady progress in New York and has to stay there for at least two weeks. Julia isn't going to fly in and do the Nurse Nightingale bit as we're going to NY ourselves next month for gigs at Fez and Joe's Pub, and we've been invited to a lot of parties and screenings here in LA. His dad lives there and picked him up from the airport. He'll be fine.

Julia has offered to pay me $20 every day to take Muttley to the dog park for an hour, so he can run around and exhaust himself before we go out partying all evening in the hope he'll be so knackered he won't notice that we've left him on his own.

"Why do I need $20 a day when we have a joint account?" I asked.

Julia said: "I thought the cash might come in handy and make you feel like you were actually earning some money. Well, you don't have anything else to do and it would really help me as I'm so busy at the moment."

I find it quite relaxing sitting under the shade of the old oak tree contemplating the meaning of life as Muttley frolics happily with the other dogs.

Muttley is definitely the friendliest, nicest dog in the pack. I feel very protective of him when the other dogs pick on him or won't let him join in the fun. The dogs in the doggy park and on our street have different personalities, much like humans.

There was an incident on our street last week between Moira's golden retriever, Henry Kissinger, and Suzanne's pit bull, Mary, following an argument over a tennis ball. Henry needed fourteen stitches in his shoulder.

Moira was completely cool about it and said it was simply a revenge attack because Henry did the same thing to Mary a year ago and now they're quits and, anyway, Mary is a Gemini. Julia would be distraught if anything ever happened to Muttley. Luckily he steers clear of any trouble being the coward that he is.

Moira said: "Would you do me a favor? I need someone to collect a package from an address in Beverly Hills and deliver it to Hollywood for me."

Moira runs a messenger service, as well as being an agent

for photographers and stylists, and had been let down by one of her regular drivers.

"What was his excuse for not turning up for work?" I asked.

"His wife hid his car keys as a punishment for staying out all night. I hate to ask but this is an emergency."

I said: "If you can work through chemo it's the least I can do."

"I insist on paying you," she said.

"Well, if you twist my arm," I said. At last I have honest employment. Julia will be so proud.

It was much easier to collect and deliver the package than I thought it would be, so I readily agreed when Moira asked me to help her out for the rest of the day, especially as she said she paid top rates and would give me a walkie-talkie to keep in touch with base. "Roger and out." I really had to say that!

I lost count of the number of times I lost my way and had to ask base control for directions. It was very stressful. People weren't in to receive packages when they said they would be or they gave the wrong addresses. Then I left an important package with the front desk instead of handing it directly to a journalist at a TV station and that caused all sorts of problems.

I recognized the name of the journalist on the package. It was the crazy woman who said I was in her space at the *Vanity Affair* Oscar Party. She was the last person in the world that I wanted to know I was now delivering mail.

I said to Moira: "I left clear instructions with the receptionist where the package needed to go."

She said: "You clearly weren't clear enough. The journalist shouted at me, so you'll have to call her back and explain where the package is."

I called her and pretended to be Australian. I'm pretty

confident that I got away with it although she did ask me if I was English.

I was hot, thirsty, and very bad-tempered indeed by the time I got the parking ticket on Sunset Boulevard, because I hadn't noticed the sign which said don't park here between the hours of 3 and 5 P.M.

After nine long hours spent delivering or collecting seventeen packages, I was exhausted. I didn't tell Moira about the parking ticket as I didn't want her to know that I was crap at the job. I stood before her with my head bowed as she severely reprimanded me for not getting signatures for the packages I'd left.

Moira totted up how much I'd earned and proudly handed me a check for $43, including $6 for petrol. Once I've paid the $50 parking fine, I'll be $7 in the red. I can't afford to work.

I miss the buzz and excitement of a TV newsroom. Newsrooms, especially the gallery where the programs are directed from, can get pretty hairy. One particular director, though extremely good at her job, was renowned for her colorful language.

So the director says to the floor manager as they were framing the shot of the interviewee while another report was being broadcast: "Tell the cunt in the purple frock to move to the right a bit."

Someone had forgotten to cut the sound from the gallery to the studio. There was a stunned silence in the gallery as the Archbishop of Canterbury asked: "Does she mean me?"

There's a chance I won't have to work again as long as I live if Julia keeps her current success rate up. She had a song in *Third Watch*★ last month. Now "Lock and Key" is being

★ London's Burning

used in the JC Penney* ad campaign. It's the one where a couple are rushing around searching for the car keys while JC Penney staff are filling the house with baby stuff. You think she's gone into labor and they're off to the hospital, but they actually go to the airport to pick up a toddler they are adopting from China.

Julia doesn't get to see a cent of the $120,000 Mr. Penney has paid for the song as all the money goes to her previous record company and music publisher. She's been told one of her new songs is going to be in a film. I was excited, but Julia told me: "I won't believe it until I'm sitting in the cinema listening to me singing my song as the credits roll and reveal my name, while at the same time holding a copy of the soundtrack CD with my song on it in one hand and eating popcorn with the other."

The TV Producer who made the *Room Mates* pilot invited Julia and me to a screening of *It Conquered Hollywood,* a terrific documentary his company has made about Sam Arkoff and Jim Nicholson who came to Hollywood in 1955 with no money, no scripts, and no stars, but that didn't stop them from making five hundred forgettable films including *I Was A Teenage Werewolf, The She Creature,* and *Bucket of Blood.* They became kings of the "B" movie industry.

The TV Producer didn't mention the demise of *Room Mates.* I have learned the hard way that in Hollywood silence means no.

Julia and I went to the after-screening party at Trader Vic's. I hadn't intended to drink any alcohol but the waiters brought out gigantic tureens of Scorpion, a cocktail made from fruit juices, almond essence, and every spirit you've ever heard of.

* C & A.

Now under normal circs I wouldn't have touched a drop of such a lethal concoction but inside the buckets of hooch were half a dozen two foot long straws; the idea being that everyone gets to know each other as they slurp the Scorpion.

This was the ideal opportunity to test Mia's straw theory. Twice I missed my mouth and the straw went up my nose. I poked myself in the eye with it three times and scratched my cheek with the end, quite badly, as I turned to listen to Julia who wanted to tell me that I was making way too much noise. Suffice to say, I didn't attract the man of my dreams and Julia had to stop the car on Pico so I could be sick. We now call it Puco. I am never going to drink Scorpions again.

36

A Sick Cosmic Joke

I was on my way to the baby shop to buy a gift for a couple who'd invited Julia (Plus One) to celebrate their baby's baptism when a man stopped me on Main Street. It was really busy and there were hundreds of people walking by, yet he stopped me.

He was Indian—a Sikh with a turban and long beard. He said: "You are very lucky."

That was enough to guarantee my attention. He said: "You are going to travel next month. You look rich, act rich, and people think you are rich but you are not. All that is going to change. Next month amazing things are going to happen to you that will change your life."

He scribbled something on a piece of paper, screwed it up into a ball, and put it in my hand.

"What's your favorite flower?"

"Lily."

"Do you have a brother or sister?"

"You're the clairvoyant, you tell me."

"Which country would you most like to visit?"

"Australia."

"What do you wish for?"

I thought for a moment: "A good man who's rich and a well paid job, please."

"Soon," he said, "soon."

He asked me to unfold my hand, take the piece of paper out, and read out loud: "Lily, A for Australia, and a brother and a sister." He'd written it before I told him the answers!

He said: "You are a very lucky person indeed. When you are a millionaire and pass me on Main Street again you should remember me. You can give me some cash now if you like."

I opened my purse and took out $20 (I didn't want to look cheap). He said: "If you give me the other $20 as well, you'll have even more luck." So I did. I need all the luck I can get. I'm feeling very underachieved.

As he shook me warmly by the hand he said: "Don't cut your hair or nails on a Tuesday and have a ring made using this stone. The setting must be solid gold, not silver."

"Can I have your card so I can call you if your predictions come true?" I asked.

He said: "You cannot contact me. I am a yogi from the Golden Temple in India and I'm just passing through."

I walked on—without looking back.

I thought Julia would be very impressed with the story as she's into all that stuff but she said: "If he was a proper yogi like Paramahansa Yogananda he would never do tricks and he certainly wouldn't ask for money. You've been had."

We were late for the baptism party but I didn't care. All I could think about was my true love and my personal bank account that would soon be overflowing instead of over-drawn.

We sat down at an empty table and did a discreet reccy of our fellow guests. No celebrities but plenty of very nice people. The grandmother of the baby being baptized, an Italian New Yorker, told us how proud she is of her family and how glad that she waited until she married her husband before she had sex with him. "Three years we waited until he'd finished medical school!" she said.

I said: "I wouldn't want to wait until I married a man before I slept with him in case he was a lousy lover."

She said: "Luckily my husband was a wonderful lover and so, as it turned out, was I!" He'd been her only lover and she was glad about that too. She said that the waiting and being faithful to each other had made their marriage all the more special.

I didn't tell her any of my sausage/honey pot stories. Suddenly they seemed rather diminished by comparison. Just then . . . the most handsome, kind, charming, witty, delightful, gorgeous man with the nicest smile stood over me and asked if he could join our table. If lightning had struck at that very moment, I wouldn't have been at all surprised.

He talked about the theatre and his television show. I normally avoid actors like Ebola fever but was prepared to make an exception in his case. I hung onto his every word.

Julia whispered: "Make sure he knows you're interested in him."

I couldn't have been more flirtatious and practically threw myself at him. "So how long have you been an actor?" I asked.

He was shocked: "Oh, I'm not an actor. I'm a priest. A Catholic priest."

"A celibate Roman Catholic priest?"

"Yes."

"Why aren't you wearing your priestly garb?"

"I'm one of the godfathers and technically off duty."

"Bugger."

Radio Ga-Ga

Julia and I always reward ourselves with tea and cake after exercise. As we ate our pumpkin and walnut loaf following a bike ride to Marina Del Rey, we mused on how hard it is to find a decent bloke who isn't either broke, narcissistic, or disappoints in the trouser department. "If they are good and kind there's no chemistry and if there's chem they are usually self-absorbed arseholes, married to someone else or hung like a cashew nut," I said.

I blame Julia for all the cake we eat. She loves it and has a slice every day. The trouble is she has willpower and sticks to one slice while I have two or three. I'd rather not have it in the house at all. As we crammed the last few cake crumbs into our mouths, I said: "If I didn't live with you I wouldn't have cake."

She replied: "If you didn't live with me you wouldn't have a roof." Ha bloody ha. I pretended to laugh but I'm actually feeling quite vulnerable and inadequate at the moment. I always imagined I'd be the one with the manager keeping the wolf from my kid sister's door. What if being repulsed when watching your own flesh and blood brush her teeth is a deal breaker for Julia and she wants me to move out? She's already mentioned that Boyfriend has excellent bathroom etiquette.

Later, over lunch with the Transformational Clairvoyant who I hadn't seen since Pink Witches night, I pondered why I seem to attract only emotionally unavailable men. "The last man I fancied was a Catholic priest, for God's sake."

She said thoughtfully: "As a Catholic priest is the ultimate unavailable man, you may at last have broken your pattern." Like the yogi, she thinks Mr. Right is just around the corner. "He's probably right under your nose," she said.

"Hallelujah!"

"But," she continued, "don't rule out the possibility of a roll in the hay with the priest. I counsel many women who've had affairs with Catholic priests."

"I like a challenge," I said, "but I do have boundaries and I don't think it's worth the risk of burning in hell."

There are more pressing matters to deal with. Julia and I need to go on a shopping spree before our trip to New York. Julia is playing some gigs there in the hope of sealing a new record deal, but it's a bit chilly in New York so we must invest in winter shoes and sweaters. New shoes means a new hand-bag—a Kate Spade. Not a real one, a copy for $25. Naomi told me you can buy them Downtown and you really can't tell the difference. Perhaps even a new coat with the money I've saved by buying a Kate Spade copy.

Mum and Dad are meeting us in New York. Dad has bought a map of the area and calls us four or five times a day to let us know that he has located the hotel and venues where Julia is playing and the quickest route to them from 42nd Street.

I was really excited about the New York trip until my mother told me on the phone that she has two wishes: that my brother will stop smoking and that I will achieve success in my own right.

"Mum, I am very happy with my life. Julia and I are a team. We like living together and, actually, I have been quite successful in my own right."

"You've spent most of your life skivvying* after other people. Start making yourself a priority for a change and put your needs ahead of others."

Skivvying? You don't live in the land of therapy for almost a year without getting into the habit of analyzing everything anyone says to you. Mum was projecting disappointment with her own life.

I inherited my nurturing and homemaking skills from my mother and my positive attitude and sense of humor came from Dad. I remember the time we were looking after a piano for some friends and were surprised to hear someone tickling the ivories, as none of us play. We rushed into the living room to find Dad stark naked at the piano à la Monty Python. We thought it was hilarious. Mum didn't and demanded that Dad "stop seeking attention."

This is very much a low budget, no frills, mini-tour of the East Coast. Mum and Dad get a hotel room but I'm sleeping on the settee of a friend of Julia's manager. Julia is staying with Boyfriend who has a place in NY as well as LA—very convenient. Julia seems quite taken by him.

His arm is still in a brace but is responding well to rehab. It's put a stop to his knuckle cracking. He never complains about the pain, which is just as well as we're not very patient with whingers.

He is an ardent Knicks fan. And, like many New Yorkers,

---

* From the noun "skivvy": a female domestic servant.

he calls his friends "Man." Despite these minor faults, he is handsome, has his own hair and teeth, no children to support from a previous marriage, never runs out of Earl Grey at his apartment, and lives just around the corner; that's where I'd like him to stay living.

Julia is getting a tad nervous about the New York trip as such a lot is resting on it. A record company has expressed a serious interest in signing her and is sending a top executive to the gigs, which, incidentally, Julia is funding herself.

It's really hard to make it in the music business. According to Sound-Scan, the independent research firm that monitors record sales in America, of the 6,188 albums released last year, only fifty sold more than a million copies. Sixty-five sold 500,000 and 356 sold 100,000. There's a 90 percent failure rate. Few recording artists release more than three albums in their musical career, so I think Julia has done really well, having released a magnificent six.

Judith, meanwhile, has suffered a bitter blow. She had been signed by a subsidiary of a major record label, which is currently undergoing a complete management restructure. The man who signed her has been sacked, which usually means that his replacement won't want to release a record that was somebody else's idea. Those records, called Flush Puppies in the industry, often don't get released at all and gather dust on a shelf somewhere, so Judith is going to buy the record back and find another home for it.

Record company executives who lose their jobs receive a massive pay off, despite usually never have written a song in their lives. If an artist is dropped or their record isn't released for whatever reason, they commonly don't receive a penny and are rarely given their record back. The vast majority can't afford to buy it back. It infuriates Julia that the executives earn a fortune and fly everywhere first class while most musicians don't earn enough to pay their rent and travel in a cramped bus.

I offered to record Julia's new songs on my Sony Walkman and then sell them on the Internet but Julia told me that only 2 percent of all records are sold on the Internet. It's better to get a proper record deal as they carry more weight in the industry and music publishers prefer it if their artists are signed to a record label.

Pity, I rather fancied myself as a record company executive. The yogi did say that I'm going to have a successful business.

38

Where Do I Sign?

We were hopeful that the New York gigs would sell out, thus creating an electric atmosphere that would inspire Julia to sing her socks off and wow the audience and the record company. But she had a hellishly bad stroke of luck in the timing department.

The week of her NY gigs coincided with two local teams of grown men slugging it out in a game of rounders, or baseball, as Americans like to call it, in a competition known as the World Series. It's laughingly called the World Series despite the fact that only American teams are eligible.

Imagine the Montagues versus the Capulets, the Jets versus the Sharks, or 1940s Germany versus the Rest of the World and you'll come somewhere near the level of tension in New York between Yankees and Mets fans. So much so that, incredibly, the hottest tickets in town were not to one of Julia's gigs at Fez or Joe's Pub on Lafeyette Street.

As if that wasn't bad enough, the Lady Record Company Executive we were hoping would sign Julia had decided to fly to Hawaii on the day of the first gig and would now miss it. Julia couldn't believe her bad luck: "All this effort and expense to impress one woman and she isn't even coming now."

I saved the day by suggesting the Lady Record Company Executive come to a rehearsal instead, which she agreed to. I promised to be on my best behavior.

I liked the Lady Record Company Executive as soon as she walked into the room as she was warm and friendly, unusual traits in record company executives. She made me feel so at ease that I felt confident enough to do that thing that salesmen do to make them sound caring and you important by saying your name at the end of every sentence.

After I'd called her Cathy about twenty-six times (Welcome Cathy. Can I take your coat Cathy? Would you like a cup of tea Cathy?), Julia asked me, in a voice full of shame and embarrassment, why I kept calling Karen, Cathy?

The Lady Record Company Executive saw the funny side and said that she loved the new songs and definitely wanted to sign Julia. Phew!

As we left the rehearsal studio I asked Julia: "Why aren't you jumping up and down with joy?"

She said: "Just because a record company says it wants to sign you doesn't mean that it will. It ain't final 'til it's vinyl."

I added: "I see. No time for glee 'til it's a CD."

I prayed every day that TLRCE wouldn't come to a sticky end in America's fiftieth state.

The gigs were a huge success. A critic at the *Washington Post* said of Julia's performance at the Birchmere ". . . a remarkable singer—her voice frequently glided between angelic flourishes and sultry moans without a hitch . . . also displayed her considerable talents as a jazz balladeer and composer . . ."

The best gig of the mini-tour was the fourth one at Joe's Pub. Despite the fact that it was the deciding game in the World Series, it was a sell out—a triumph for Julia and the Yankees. I didn't do so badly myself. A friend introduced me to the Record Producer with whom I enjoyed a wonderful brief encounter.

His marriage was long. The divorce expensive. No kids. He looked like a cross between Steven Seagal and Harvey Keitel. He played me his favorite music (Puccini) and read me poetry (Kenneth Rexroth). He makes a perfect cup of tea—leaves, not tea bags. I didn't feel a need to try to be funny and there were many comfortable silences—a novelty for me. I liked the sound of his voice. The way he said my name.

It was a bit tricky keeping my brief encounter a secret from Mum and Dad. I had to eat dinner twice a night, once with the parents and then again with the Record Producer. And as I wasn't getting to sleep until very late, I kept nodding off during the day much to Julia's and Mum and Dad's irritation.

The trouble with holiday romances is that they rarely blossom into anything permanent.

The Record Producer said, as we bid each other farewell: "How often do you visit New York, because I hate LA?"

"Once every ten years and it's a very long walk from New York to LA," I said.

He nodded. "I'll call you."

Yeah right.

When we got back to LA, Julia and I went to see *The Vagina Monologues* at the Canon Theatre with some American girlfriends who all brought their mothers along. This was astonishing to Julia and me as we would never bring our dear mother to a show that featured the word vagina, let alone the "C" word.

We met for an early dinner at Spago, the trendy restaurant opposite the theatre. When I say trendy, I mean expensive. We managed to find a bottle of wine that cost less than $300, a pleasant enough Pinot Noir for $46. As if ordering a bottle of "cheap" wine wasn't enough to disgust our waiter, asking to share appetizers was the final straw. He hated us.

Our main topic of conversation was girlie toilet parts. Suzanne's mother wanted to know what we all called our vaginas when we were young—"Mouse," "Cookie," "Schmekle," "Petey," "Pussycat," "Pooky." Then it was our turn. Julia and I bowed our heads and twiddled our napkins in embarrassment: "Private," we whispered. Howls of laughter. Suzanne's mother asked sweetly: "Is that a gentile thing?"

By this time the restaurant had filled to capacity. Sydney Poitier came in and caused quite a stir. But not as big a stir as when four of our party shrieked in unison when they spotted a man sitting at a table in the corner: "Oh my God. There's my gynecologist!"

39

Hair Today, Gone Tomorrow

Have you ever wondered why Meg Ryan's hair looks like a million dollars? It's because that's how much it costs.

As she is soon to sign a new record deal, Julia has decided that she needs a "do" that befits an international recording artist. To this end, she called the salon of one Sally Hershberger at John Frieda. Ms. Hershberger charges the likes of Meg Ryan *and* ordinary housewives a whopping $500 a cut.

The receptionist who handled Julia's request for an appointment within the next week laughed mockingly at the absurdity of it and offered the services of Freddy who has been personally trained by Miss Hershberger and charges a mere $300.

After much agonizing, Julia decided to pay the $300. I said: "Call back and make sure they understand you just want Freddy to cut your hair, not shag you as well."

Freddy didn't get off to a good start in my book by holding up bits of Julia's hair and inspecting it as if it was something stuck to his shoe that Muttley had done. He said: "I will transform her from a suburban housewife into a goddess."

And by jove he did. He even gave her hair extensions so she left the salon with longer hair than she went in with. I said: "Keep your hair on!" at every opportunity over the next three days.

Freddy was worth every penny. Julia looked amazing. We went straight out and bought a flat iron so we could achieve the same effect at home. What with the expense of that and all the new John Frieda hair products, she spent way more than $500 but she did look great.

Now the trouble with a Meg Ryan/Cameron Diaz "do" that looks so natural and easy is that they are anything but. They are impossible to re-create at home. After three hours locked in the bathroom with the flat iron and her hair extensions, Julia came out looking like a scarecrow. She looked even worse after I had a go.

I offered to take Muttley to the dog park while Julia sorted out her hair. I saw a lovely shady spot by a massive tree but decided against sitting under it when I did a quick calculation and estimated that several thousand dogs have probably peed there. That's many gallons.

I opened Suze Orman's book, *The Courage to Be Rich,* and began to learn how to create a life of material and spiritual abundance . . .

I glanced up to check on my charge and saw Muttley attempting to mount a dog that was twice his size. This was the first time I had witnessed him trying to have his wicked way with another hound. He's sniffed a few butts in his time but he's never tried to go all the way. I shouted: "Hey, Muttley. You should at least wait until you are formally introduced and then take her out for dinner before you pounce on her."

A handsome stranger said: "Muttley, meet Georgia Brown." Muttley was clearly smitten. So was I. I momentarily took my eye off the prize when I saw Muttley take a dump in the distance. I did the honorable thing and went to scoop. I searched and searched but couldn't see it anywhere.

A voice said confidently: "You're standing in it."

I said: "I hate it when that happens."

He held out his hand for me to shake: "Hello. I'm Richard."

Before I could say "Best in Show," I'd passed him the bag of Muttley's poo instead of shaking his hand.

I said: "I hate it when that happens."

He laughed and suggested we sit on the bench. He told me how he had never been a dog person but had found Georgia as a puppy whimpering in an old oil drum. He said, "I took her to an animal rescue place and called a few days later to see how she was doing. They said she was going to be put down the next day if they hadn't found a home for her so I took her in. That was three years ago."

Handsome and kind. A winning combination.

"So what do you do?" I asked.

"I'm a musician," he said.

I said: "How interesting."

I thought: "What do you call a musician without a girl-friend? Answer: Homeless."

We watched Muttley and sweet Georgia Brown frolic joyfully until a German shepherd called Colin (after Colin Powell) bounded over to muscle in on Muttley's action.

The Muttster didn't stand a chance. He bravely growled at Colin who responded with the canine equivalent of an upper cut, then pinned Muttley to the ground. Muttley was limping badly and could hardly walk back to the car. I struggled to lift him, but he weighs a whopping 59 pounds so Georgia's dad carried him for me. I glared at Colin Powell's owner who looked the other way.

I said: "I'd better take him to the vet."

"Do you want me to come with you?" he asked.

"That's okay. Thanks. We'll be fine," I said. I do not need another impoverished gentleman caller.

There are 500,000 Brits living in LA and many of them choose to give their beloved pet a name that reminds them fondly of home so I didn't flinch when the veterinary nurse called out: "Flea powder for Cilla Black"?* My favorite is Delia Smith.† She's mostly Chihuahua with just a hint of fruit bat.

"Are you Muttley's mother?" asked the vet.

"No, I'm his aunt." The vet continued to push, pull, and prod Muttley's hind legs.

"Be gentle with him," I pleaded.

"No broken bones. He's just a bit bruised. I think he may have a touch of arthritis so you should buy him a coat to keep his legs warm."

I let Muttley sit with me in the front of the car as we drove home and stroked his back, just like I did to my own kids when they were sick. Muttley seemed to like it. It was the moment that I realized that Muttley really is one of the family. I never imagined that I'd ever think fondly of the four-legged freak of nature from Fiji.

Much to my surprise, Julia was all for the coat idea. I said: "He's going be a laughingstock to the dogs on the street and he'll probably get beaten up at doggy park again by Colin Powell." But Julia ignored my protests and bought him a red outfit. Bright red.

Muttley actually likes wearing it and red certainly does suit him. Julia wants him to wear it when we pose for our

---

* Kathi Lee Gifford.
† Martha Stewart.

Christmas photo. We are to wear matching red sweaters with tinsel draped over our shoulders. For fuck's sake!

That afternoon at ladies tea, Suzanne told us that she'd gone away with an old boyfriend to a fancy hotel for a weekend to celebrate his birthday. They took the boyfriend's beloved dog with them. Well, the dog was struck down by something called "bloat" and had to have costly emergency surgery to save its life. Suzanne described the weekend thus: "I blew my boyfriend, the dog blew up, and my boyfriend blew three and a half thousand bucks."

Judith had some good news to share. She is to feature on *The Simpsons* as a cartoon character. She said: "It will look exactly like me with long blond hair and a pointy nose. She'll be singing one of my songs, which means lovely royalties every time it broadcasts around the world and now I own the record all the money comes to me!"

The Record Producer continues to call me three times a day, sometimes for two hours, and always last thing at night. He likes to read me poetry. I'm not sure if he's being romantic or just likes the sound of his own voice. He did mention that he'd like to try his hand at acting. I've nearly dropped off to sleep a couple of times mid sonnet. Julia says it's significant that he calls me last thing at night and it means that he must really like me and isn't sleeping with anyone else. Moira said he's produced lots of hit records so must be very rich, which would explain the huge Riverside apartment that's overflowing with antiques and why he doesn't appear worried about his phone bill.

Moira asked us to go with her for her first acupuncture session. "I'm doing some alternative therapy as well as the chemo but I hate needles and could do with some moral support."

"Of course we'll come," we chorused.

Which is how Julia, Suzanne, Naomi, Judith, and I were sitting around Moira's bed as a Chinese doctor stuck pins in her, singing at the tops of our voices: "Healings. Nothing more than healings." Followed by the old Searchers hit "Needles and Pins."

Dr. Ping was soon joining in, wonderfully out of tune. He was having trouble sticking a needle in Moira's groin, so I said: "Is it like looking for a needle in a haystack?"

Dr. Ping turned around laughing: "What's your point? Funny, no?"

If laughter is the best medicine, Moira should be repaired by Christmas.

40

Minus One

Mia is pulling pints at the Hogshead for pocket money while she's contemplating her future, having passed her hairdressing course with distinction. I don't like her working so many hours in a smoky atmosphere but she needs to earn quite a bit to pay for her nicotine habit and beer money.

Yesterday a stranger walked into the pub and asked for a pint of Hoegaarden. She was able to tell him that the Belgian beer is flavored with coriander and orange peel and pulled his pint perfectly, with just the right amount of head. (Oh, pleeeeease!)

When he'd finished sipping his ale, the man called her over and told her that he worked for Hoegaarden and was carrying out spot-checks throughout the southwest of England to see if local barmaids knew about the beer and how to pour it.

He was delighted to present her with a certificate announcing that she had passed the Hoegaarden Challenge, the first barmaid in the Southwest to achieve the honor. As well as the certificate, she received $15 in gift vouchers and $20 in cash.

The landlord was so pleased and proud that he had the

certificate framed and it now hangs prominently behind the bar. Mia placed two candles and a teddy bear on a shelf in front it and made it into a shrine. The customers call her the Hoegaarden Queen. That's my girl!

Max wasn't impressed with his sister's achievement at all but did want to know where to apply for the spot-checker's job.

Julia has flown back to London for her green card interview at the American Embassy. Her immigration lawyer says that it's just a formality because she is "an alien of extraordinary ability." Julia says it's a pain in the arse.

She doesn't understand why she can't do the interview here. I think it's because America doesn't want to make it too easy for people to get green cards or everyone will want one. I'm just an "alien of exceptional ability" by the way, which, apparently, isn't as important as "extraordinary."

Julia wants a green card so she doesn't have to go through the rigmarole of renewing her visa every year. The trouble with getting a green card is that Brits have to start paying taxes in America as well as the UK. The lawyer's fees are about $5,000 to get a green card and the process can take three years. And although it's a card, it's not even green.

But once you've got one, you can go for U.S. Citizenship, which only costs about $200 and you get to keep your British passport. It's not any easier if you marry an American either. It can still take three years and you really do have to pass the green card interview. One of the advantages with being a U.S. citizen is that it's easier to get family members into the country for an extended stay.

Judith got hers last week. She had to swear allegiance to the American flag at the Staples Center, along with six thousand other people, in a moving ceremony that was over in ten seconds. We had a party to celebrate and played "Guess the British TV Theme."

Clive, a British actor chum of Moira's was in charge of the CD and acted as referee. The Americans couldn't understand why we Brits got so excited when the *Crossroads* theme tune came on. They were even more perplexed when I uttered the immortal name "Amy Turtle"* and the other Brits all sighed nostalgically. We were like coiled springs, desperate to be the first to remember if it was the Saint or the Persuaders. Tales of the Unexpected! We got our Thunderbirds mixed up with our Stingray and many a nostalgic tear was shed over Steptoe and Son.

And who could forget "The Horse of the Year Show?" Everyone except me, that's who. Which is why I won the tiebreaker and scooped the first prize—a Mars bar. Again the Americans were nonplussed. Boyfriend asked: "How can anyone get so excited about a Mars bar? How could any country have a program called 'The Horse of the Year Show'?"

I turned to Judith and whispered: "How can any country think a pretzel's worth eating?"

She said: "Fair point, well made." The Brits all started feeling terribly homesick.

We were snapped out of our malaise when Clive's mother reminded us why she was planning to move to LA from London permanently. This is a formidable woman whose son affectionately calls her Lady Pearse. Not because she is a member of the landed gentry but because she acts and sounds like she should be. Her voice is a cross between Lady Bracknell† and the Queen Mother.‡

---

* Elderly chambermaid on British daytime soap *Crossroads* about a Birmingham motel that was so awful it became compulsive viewing.
† Formidable character invented by Oscar Wilde in his play, *The Importance of Being Earnest*.
‡ Queen Elizabeth II's mother. Favorite British Royal who lived until the ripe old age of 101.

She said the final straw for her was to walk into her favorite restaurant and see a handwritten sign that read: "OAPs.★
Fish and Chips. $2.50." England has become too down mar-
ket, she said.

But England has much to be proud of—*The Sound of
Music* for a start. I know it was written by Americans but Julie
Andrews, a Dame of the British Empire, is the star. We ended
our evening by watching that great musical because it's
Moira's favorite film.

There was much rewinding and playing of the scene just
before the Mother Superior starts singing "Climb Every
Mountain." The Mother Superior says to Maria/Julie Andrews
who has just returned to the convent because she's fallen in
love with Baron Von Trapp: "Maria, what is it you can't face?"

In her clipped English accent it sounds as if the Mother
Superior is saying: "Maria, what is it you cunt face?" After
we'd replayed the scene fifty times and managed to stop
howling with laughter, we sang "Climb Every Mountain"
along with the Mother Superior at the tops of our voices.
Moira has adopted it as her theme song.

Julia's green card interview was not just a formality. They
wouldn't give it to her because she was missing a current police report to prove that she had never been arrested. It had
got caught up in a backlog at the Metropolitan Police and
hadn't been processed.

She has to fly back again as soon as it comes through. She
was beyond distressed and frustrated. She told me on the
phone that some people were sobbing outside the American
Embassy because they didn't get theirs and their visas had already expired so they couldn't get back into the country and
this was before September 11. This green card business can

★ Old Age Pensioner. Senior citizen.

be quite an ordeal. I think I'll stick with my "I" journalist's visa. It's valid for another four years.

I'd had a severe trial myself that morning. I took Muttley to the dog park just up the road on the corner of Pacific and Main for a change. The other two parks that I've taken him to have double gates so the dogs can't escape. Not this one. I was so shocked when a Chihuahua snuck out as I opened the gate to let Muttley in that I still didn't close it when the other owners started screaming at me to shut it and another one got out.

The owners became hysterical. The Chihuahua was caught by a young girl with a shaved head and a ring through her nose, a man jumped over the fence and chased after the husky, which was racing toward traffic. Another man jumped over the fence the other way to stop the cars. The screech of brakes was terrifying. I was so traumatized that I couldn't move. A lady in an ill-fitting shocking pink coat glared as she shut the gate for me. Not out of kindness either but because she felt superior.

The man threw himself at the husky and missed. Then, Richard, the man I met at the other dog park with his border collie, Georgia Brown, came round the corner and managed to grab the husky and no doubt saved his life. I was very distressed because the other dog owners kept shouting at me for being so stupid. "Are you crazy?"

My hero said: "She didn't do it on purpose. Give the lady a break." He called me a lady!

Muttley was oblivious to all the drama. He only had eyes for Georgia Brown. When I finally stopped trembling and got up to leave, the other owners held tightly onto their dogs while my knight in shining armor opened the gate for me. He smiled. He's got a lovely smile.

"Do you have time for a coffee?" he asked.

"Sure," I said.

He ordered a mocha. I had regular coffee with milk. HE PAID!

"How come you and Georgia haven't been to the dog park for a while?" I asked.

"The day after I met you I was asked to compose the music and a theme song for the new Scooby Doo cartoon series and spent the next two weeks trapped in a studio during the day so we went to the park in the evening. We've been going there in the day for a few days and hadn't seen you and Muttley so we've been checking out all the other parks until we found you. Georgia has been pining for Muttley. So, tell me about your children. . . ."

I was sweeping the kitchen floor for the third time that day when Julia walked in from her trip. Boyfriend had picked her up from the airport. I complained: "There's enough of your dog's hair on this floor to stuff a mattress."

Once she'd hugged Muttley and me, Julia began opening the mail. "Great," she said. "It's an invitation to the Hollywood Manager's Christmas Party."

"I'm going to buy a new dress," I said excitedly.

Julia looked embarrassed. "Actually, I'm taking Boyfriend as my Plus One."

41

A Brief Encounter

Not even a Plus One. My days in California could well be numbered. It was bad enough being usurped by a dog but to be ranked third behind Boyfriend may be too much to bear.

I thought I couldn't possibly get any more depressed until I caught a glimpse of my reflection in the kitchen window and realized that Julia was absolutely right—I have indeed chubbed up a bit. Substantially more than a bit, actually. And that's not how you want to look at my time of life with no job, no husband, and no prospects.

I pulled out the bathroom scale from the towel cupboard, dusted it off, and was appalled to discover that I had hit a personal best or, more accurately, worst weight. A number that was so shockingly high that I am unable to write the figure down or say it out loud. I didn't weigh this much when I was nine months pregnant. Not good. Not good at all.

A thorough inspection of my physique in the full length mirror confirmed my worst fear that I looked like a Bulgarian air stewardess whose only claim to fame was that she had won a bronze medal for throwing the discus in the 1992 Barcelona Olympic Games.

"Do you want to come to a BAFTA screening with me as

my Plus One on Tuesday night?" Julia asked me as I folded laundry. She had an irritating and strange expression on her face, as if she was sucking a sherbet lemon and, an almost impossible feat, at the same time smirking like she was privy to some huge secret that only she knew but might let me in on if I was very, very lucky.

"The film isn't highbrow or independent enough for Boyfriend, then?" I snarled in my best "Princess Evil of the Hideous People" voice.

"No," she said. "I'm giving you first refusal on this one."

"What film is it?"

"Some actor's directorial debut. He's doing a Q & A afterward so we might get to meet him."

Oh, fuck off with your smirking. "What's his name?"

Julia scooped up her clean underwear and walked away grinning. "George Clooney," she announced triumphantly.

The Los Angeles Symphony Orchestra began playing Carl Orff's *Carmina Burana* in my head as I did my happy dance, which is very hard to do when your legs have turned to jelly. I don't know why Julia took so long to choose an outfit to wear. It's not as if George is HER fantasy boyfriend. He is mine. All mine. And I finally have him in my grasp. I'd managed to lose five pounds in four days on a no alcohol, no wheat, no dairy, and absolutely no cake diet.

I decided to stick with media black. Black pants (Liz Claiborne), white tee shirt (Gap) and my fitted black jacket from Max Mara that Julia bought me eight years ago. It has served me very well.

The anticipation before the curtain went up was extraordinary with 75 percent of the audience craning their necks and swiveling their heads like Linda Blair in *The Exorcist,* desperate for a sneak peek at George.

I and the remaining civilized 25 percent chose to look

straight ahead or fumbled in our handbags for an imaginary tissue in a pathetic and unsuccessful attempt to look calm and in control, pretending not to care a jot if we clapped eyes on him or not.

Confessions of a Dangerous Mind was bloody good. Glory be, he isn't just a pretty face. George, My Beloved George, walked down the aisle to the stage after the film had been screened to rapturous applause. Julia and I had positioned ourselves about halfway—not too close to be sad bastards but close enough to get a good view.

There were gasps of delight as George took to the stage. Men nodded in agreement that this was indeed one handsome dude.

He handled the questions with wit and style. He is smart and funny and self-deprecating and good and kind to animals (look how devoted he is to his Vietnamese potbellied pig, Max. HIS PIG IS CALLED MAX! My son is called Max. IT'S A SIGN!).

When he answered questions from the audience, he looked his inquisitors straight in the eye in a kindly way, never averting his gaze or hinting in his tone that the question was overlong or didn't have a point or had already been answered.

Then the young woman directly in front of me, God bless her, asked him a question. Quite a good one if memory serves but not so good that I can recall it because my mind went a complete blank after George starting looking at me. I swear George was looking straight at me as he answered her. HE WAS LOOKING STRAIGHT AT ME. George HAD NOTICED ME!

It was so incredible that I could barely stand it. I had a knowing, absolute conviction that George and I were meant for each other.

Julia thinks he was looking at her but that's ludicrous. It was definitely me. George looked at me lovingly and longingly as he answered the lady's question.

No, really. HE DID! He really did. The trouble is every woman in that room wanted him and honestly believed that they were in with a shot.

Who am I kidding? It would be impossible for him to remain faithful to me, however much he wanted to. All that filming on location with the world's most beautiful and seductive actresses—he'd be bound to succumb eventually. That wicked temptress Renée Zellweger has always had the hots for him.

Let's say George and I did get married, how long, realistically, would it last? Not very long is the answer. After much deliberation and analysis of his past history and his emphatic public declarations that marriage and commitment aren't for him, I decided that, even if George proposed and I know that the chances of that are slim to none, I would have to say no. The man's a serial shagger for Christ's sake. And who can blame him?

Julia nudged me from my dream of what might have been. "Come on. Let's go to the stage and try and meet him."

"Good God, no. I have my dignity." Unlike the eighty or so other women who were scrambling for the stage and a closer look, maybe even a touch.

Julia said: "Are you crazy? This could be your one and only chance to meet your fantasy boyfriend."

But I wouldn't be budged. I left that theater with a heavy heart but my head held high. I went to the rest room to compose myself and wonder, in the privacy of my own cubicle, who might have designed my wedding gown. Vera Wang? Georgio?

I lagged behind Julia as we headed for the car and there,

in the distance, surrounded by a gaggle of preening women was George looking ridiculously handsome and being completely charming as he held court with his adoring public.

Julia grabbed my arm and gasped: "Quick, come on, here's your chance to finally meet George Clooney."

"I have no intention of humiliating myself just so I can tell everyone I know back home that I went to Hollywood and met George Clooney," I said.

"Are you insane? It's one of the main reasons you came to California in the first place! You are so stubborn, it's infuriating. Well if you won't go and introduce yourself to him, I'll do it for you." Julia mumbled some West Coast bullshit about destiny and Mercury up Uranus and marched straight up to George.

I followed sheepishly, mortified, yet also strangely excited and hid behind a nearby tree. Julia told George as she shook his hand enthusiastically: "Congratulations on making an excellent film. My sister, *Claire,* and I really enjoyed it. My sister, *Claire*, and I drove up together from Santa Monica. That's my sister, *Claire*, over there. By that tree."

George, in slowest motion, looked over at me. We stared deeply into each other's eyes for about an hour. He really is a wonder to behold. Then George Clooney, yes *the* George Clooney, smiled at me and said: "Hello, Claire."

Julia and I walked silently, hearts pounding, arms linked, to the car. Once we'd reached the motor, we carefully looked around to see if anyone could see us. As soon as we had confirmed that no one was in sight, we started screaming and jumping up and down like a pair of twelve-year-olds who had just bumped into——(insert name of current teen idol).

George didn't ask for my number or follow me back to the car but I can honestly say that I did meet him. My mission in this country is now complete.

42

Someone to Watch Over Me

Now that I know I'm not going to marry George Clooney I need to rethink my future. This trip was only meant to be for a year but I really love living in California and would like to stay but if Julia wants Boyfriend to move in, I'm royally buggered. I can't afford to set up on my own here but I wouldn't want to stand in the way of Julia's happiness.

ITN's got a new 24-hour cable news channel so there might be some graveyard shifts for me back in London. The sun does shine in England sometimes. Nineteen seventy-six was a fantastic summer. I suppose I could move to New York. I called the Record Producer to see if he was coming to see me for Christmas or New Year's. Silence.

I moped around for a bit then began flicking through the pile of mail that Julia had abandoned after opening her invitation to the Hollywood Manager's Christmas Party. Julia, who was rearranging her teapot collection, turned round to find out why I was running up and down, punching the air with my fist and shouting "yes, yes" at the top of my voice as if I'd just scored the winning goal in a World Cup Final.

I sang the first few bars of Queen's "We Are the Champions of the World" before telling her proudly (with just a hint of smugness) that I had received my own invitation to the Hollywood Manager's Christmas Party. Our celebrations were cut short by my telephone's shrill ring.

Suzanne was calling to see if I was free to make up a foursome at the Beverly Hills Tennis Club. She was sorry it was such short notice but she was playing against a TV Director who was interested in developing a show she's creating. Could I be there in half an hour? I sponged Muttley's muddy paw prints from my tennis skirt and was out the front door before you could say Martina Navratilova.

I didn't play badly at all. My forehand passing down the line was excellent and my backhand didn't suck like it normally does. Lunch was even better. I was in the gang. The TV Director, Suzanne, her agent, and me . . . chewing the fat. The TV Director said to me: "So I hear you've got a dog. . . ."

I told a few Muttley stories and marveled at how much it costs to keep a dog. "Ten grand is peanuts," he said, "my dog's got his own lawyer on a retainer!" I sat transfixed as the TV Director regaled us with some of his dog's tales.

He told us how he'd taken his beloved dog to the park near his New York apartment and the dog started sniffing a man's shoes. The man pushed him away with his foot. This enraged the TV Director who ran over and punched the man who punched him back and then the dog bit the man on the hand.

"It was just a nip," said the TV Director, "only seven stitches. But the guy sued and I had to pay him seven grand." Another time the dog went to play with the dog who lived in the apartment next door on a play date and ate the newlywed couple's couch that had been a wedding present from the bride's parents. He paid them $3,000 cash for a new one.

Then the dog bit a woman. That was $5,000. Then he attacked a man in another dog park who also sued. In New York it's a case of "three bites and you're out." The lawyer insisted on a retainer before he would take the case. "He took two identical German shepherds into the courtroom. The guy couldn't positively identify which one was my dog so the case was dismissed," said the TV Director.

I said: "But if he had identified your dog it would have been taken from court and put down."

"No it wouldn't," he said. "I would never have let that happen. I made sure that neither of the dogs that went to court were mine."

I opened the front door at the end of my memorable day to see Muttley mimicking Julia's downward dog as she completed her yoga tape. That's got to be worth ten grand of anyone's money.

I took Muttley to the dog park for his afternoon romp and was very happy to see that Georgia Brown was there. Pretty soon I was exchanging life stories with Georgia's dad.

It took him fifteen years to realize he wasn't going to be the next Jon Bon Jovi, so he stopped being the lead singer in a New York rock band and moved to LA seven years ago to seek his fortune in the music business.

"Composing the music for the new Scooby Doo animation series is my big chance," he said.

"That's great, Richard. Congratulations," I said.

"My friends call me Rich."

"Rich?"

"Is Rich okay with you?"

"Really. Rich is fine with me."

I guess I should have been more specific. The cosmos has sent me a man called Rich not a man who is rich.

"I've been invited to a party at the weekend, would you like to come with me as my Plus One?" I asked.

"Sure," said Rich.

43

Pretty Perfect

Boyfriend drove us to the party. He's had a knob fitted onto his steering wheel (oh, pleeeeease!) so he can drive one handed. Rich and I sat in the back with our knees under our chins. I used to measure success by whether parties had complimentary valet parking but I've now changed the benchmark to include having your Christmas tree professionally decorated and a resident piano player. This one accompanied Julia as she sang some of her songs.

After Julia finished singing, we wandered round the room celebrity spotting while Rich and Boyfriend went to the bar. We saw Michelle Pfeiffer and David Kelly, Jodie Foster, Stockard Channing, and Reserve Fantasy Boyfriend David Do-Shag-Me. Then I saw the Writer with a beautiful woman draped over his arm. I'd not heard from him since he went back to the UK to work on a TV show. At least he had the decency to look embarrassed. "Hello," he said. "Have you met my wife?"

"How lovely to meet you," I said, shaking her hand. "I didn't realize you were married."

"We got married when I went home to make the TV series," said the Writer.

"That's nice," I said.

The Writer said: "Ah, there's David Duchovny. Come on darling," and he dragged his wife away.

Julia looked at me in disbelief. "Did I miss a couple of chapters?" she asked.

It wasn't hard to spot the fruits of my loins walk through Arrivals at LAX Airport. Max was wearing his silliest hat. "Did you have to wear the silly hat?" I asked. Mum and Dad were flying in later for the Christmas festivities.

Max dropped his bags, opened his arms wide, and shouted to anyone who would listen: "I am not a homosexual. Just because I am wearing a hat does not mean that I am gay. Hello, Mother. How are you?"

Mia said to her brother: "For fuck's sake. You're such a wanker."

I pointed at Max: "You—stop shouting."

I pointed at Mia: "And you—stop swearing." I hate it when she swears.

I embraced them both. "Did you remember the Quality Street★ and the Marks and Spencer† Luxury Christmas Pudding?" America doesn't have everything.

The kids noticed the huge improvement in Muttley's behavior since their last trip. He didn't bark at the FedEx Man when he delivered a Christmas present from my East Coast Gentleman Caller, the Record Producer.

I opened the fur-lined box and found a string of wooden beads. Mia asked: "Did he make it himself?"

The telephone rang as I held them up for closer inspec-

★ Chocolate candy. My Mum's favorite is the one with the purple wrapper.
† The best convenience food and underwear. The store I miss the most.

tion. The clasp was definitely gold. It was the Record Producer. "Yes," I said. "It has arrived. Thank you so much. They're
lovely. . . . Really?"

I thanked him again and said to Mia: "It's Roman. Two
thousand years old. Must have cost a small fortune."

She eyed the necklace more keenly: "Rich eh? How old
is he?"

"Fifty-six."

"He might be old but rich is good."

I said: "Fifty-six is not old but we don't want a man who
sends us expensive presents. We want a man who wants to be
with us. Love is more important than money."

Mia said: "Love AND money works though, right?"

"Oh yes, my child."

44

What's Your Point, Caller?

Max and Mia woke me on Christmas morning at five by spread-eagling their bodies over me. "I'm a human blanket," they cried. "I'm a human blanket." They haven't done that since they were four and six.

They had already opened their Christmas stockings and eaten their Terry's Chocolate Oranges, jelly bellies, M&M's, and walnuts. Much to my surprise and delight, they presented me with a stocking that was overflowing with gifts, all beautifully wrapped.

My eyes filled with tears. This was the first Christmas stocking they'd ever given me. My mind drifted to the Christmas stockings of my youth, which always included a bar of Cadbury's Fruit & Nut chocolate and a pair of American tan tights. Happy days.

But this stocking was really special. I slowly opened the first gift, savoring every moment. It was a half empty bottle of Clinique moisturizer. Then came a recently opened bottle of Clarins Eau Dynamisante, my favorite perfume. A potato. A carrot. A sprout. An empty wrapper from a Terry's Chocolate Orange. One of Julia's CDs. A cotton bud. My toothbrush.

"Very funny," I said and soon joined in their howls of laughter.

I usually refuse all offers of help in the kitchen (Controlling? *Moi?*), but there was so much food to prepare for Christmas lunch that it was a case of all hands on deck. It was quite the happy bonding experience as Julia, Max, Mia, and I peeled and chopped. Even Boyfriend helped cook with his one good hand.

The happy and calm atmosphere was a welcome relief. Earlier, Max had advised Mia to stop eating so many tortilla chips, which she interpreted as a dig at her weight, which means war. She said: "Fuck off."

He called her a bitch. She poked her tortilla chip covered tongue out at him and called out: "Mum he tried to French kiss me." I came in to intervene but they were both laughing. "Just messing with your mind, Mum."

I begged the children not to swear in front of Mum. I told Max and Mia that I was deadly serious and offered them $50 each if they managed to make it through Christmas without offending the parents. We shook on it.

I gave the kids a pleading look as Mum and Dad arrived. They are staying in a nearby apartment as our inn is full. Mum was soon showing everyone her new Christmas handbag from Dad. "It's a Kate Spade," she said proudly.

I looked at Dad. "Twenty-five bucks from Downtown?"

Dad nodded. "Thanks for the tip."

Max assured me that everything would go without a hitch as he took Mum and Dad's coats to Julia's bedroom. Mum was soon practicing her scales at the piano and having a bit of trouble reaching top A. Julia explained how she had to start low and work her way up. Soon they were both hitting top A and I was developing a headache.

I signaled to Max and Mia to stop giggling as Julia taught

Mum some of her more dramatic voice exercises, which may be good for the vocal chords but look and sound completely ridiculous.

Earlier, I had witnessed Julia kissing Boyfriend under the mistletoe after he gave her a Christmas card. He had written: "You are the angel my Mom always said would come." This could be serious. They've even got pet names for each other but Julia won't let me tell you what they are. He's going over to talk to Dad. Sweet Jesus, don't let him ask Dad for permission to marry her.

Julia came over and teased me for putting "compulsory garnish" on every plate. I said: "Please note that I am holding a sharp knife and taking estrogen so you might like to hold the sarcasm."

"I've been thinking," I continued nervously, "my year in California is almost up and you seem to be getting on very well with Boyfriend so I was wondering if maybe it's time for me to move out so he can move in here with you. You might want to start a family of your own."

"Are you crazy? I love living with you and Muttley." She looked proudly from Muttley to me and back to Muttley. "I live with my beloved sister and my dog. You are my family. I've got a lovely boyfriend who lives around the corner. Why would I want to change things? We don't want anyone else moving in here and spoiling our perfect life. I love you and your compulsory garnish. Before you came, it was just me and a packet of frozen veggie burgers."

I gave a "thumbs up" sign to the cosmos.

Julia said: "Go on admit it, you've fallen in love with Muttley, haven't you?"

"I might love Muttley a bit but I am definitely not IN love with him," I said.

"I know he's a freak of nature but I'm in love with him

and I don't care who knows it. Look at that face. I could eat it with a spoon. Have you ever seen a more handsome hound?" asked Muttley's mother. "He's a treasure on four legs spreading his joy all over the world."

Boyfriend didn't ask Dad for Julia's hand. He asked Dad to explain the rules of cricket. Nice suck up.

I noticed Mum deep in conversation with my children so I nervously picked up a glass of champagne and went over to join them just in time to hear Mum ask Max: "Tell me dear, why did you break up with your girlfriend? She was such a nice girl."

He said solemnly: "She brought up the 'C' word once too often, I'm afraid."

Mia asked, perplexed: "What? Cunt?"

My champagne glass shattered into a million pieces as it hit the floor.

I gasped: "He meant commitment." And waited for all hell to break loose.

Mum said: "Have any of you seen *The Sopranos?* Your grandfather and I love it. They say fuck and pussy a lot but it's really rather good, don't you think?"

As I carried the magnificent, organically reared turkey from Wild Oats to the table, which had been royally stuffed with American Turkey Stuffing (p. 193, *Delia Smith's Christmas*), I looked around the room at my family. Julia had never looked so radiant. She held up an official looking document and said: "This is my new recording contract. I wanted you all to be here when I signed it. This has been a great year for me. I have a sister, a boyfriend, the world's most precious dog, and now some nice people are going to give me cash to make another record."

We all clinked our glasses as Julia signed the contract. Dad assumed position to photograph the momentous occasion. The family groaned as Dad said: "No talking. This is a silent film."

Mum said: "Do you think you could make a new year's resolution to stop saying 'no talking this is a silent film' every time you take a photograph. Forty-five years he's been saying it. Forty-five years!"

I asked: "When do you think the photographs will be ready, Dad?"

He burst into song: "Some day your prints will come!"

"Stop attention seeking," demanded Mum.

While Dad was framing the shot, something that takes an inordinate amount of time, there was a knock at door. If this was a true Hollywood Story, I'd have opened the door to George Clooney but this has been a true Santa Monica story. I had to kiss an awful lot of frogs but, thanks to the fat dog from Fiji, I finally found a potential prince.

I looked on nervously as Mum watched Rich greet everyone. She is quick to judge and her first impression of one of Julia's or my boyfriends is always final. She smiled and winked at me. Max and Mia went up to Rich and shook hands with him. They said in their best cute kid voices: "Are you going to be our new daddy?"

Rich gave them each a dollar and said: "Here's your pocket money, kids. Now go outside and play. And don't do drugs."

"Thanks Dad."

Mum said: "He'll do very nicely."

She cut straight to the chase and began his interview: "How old are you?"

"Thirty-seven."

"Have you been married before?"

"No."

"Why not?"

"Hadn't met the right woman."

"Do you want children?"

He said: "No thanks."

To which Mum replied: "Well, if you decide you do want a child of your own, she could have fertility treatment. There's a doctor in Italy who can make women in their sixties pregnant."

Julia and I stared at each other aghast. I kissed Rich on the cheek and said: "That will never happen." I nodded toward Max and Mia who were throwing peanuts up in the air and catching them in their mouths. "But I could make you a grandfather."

I came to California a year ago seeking excitement, thinking that I had nothing and my life was boring and discovered that I actually have everything I need right here within the bosom of my wonderfully flawed but loving and secure family. Like my own mother, my destiny is to be the heartbeat of my own precious little unit.

My future looks pretty damn good. I have a really nice boyfriend and I've even made a big dent in my overdraft thanks to my new career as a professional dog walker. People pay me $20 to take their precious pets to the dog park for an hour. My rapidly expanding business is called "Claire's Puppy Love." It needs to expand so I can take out a bank loan and buy a truck. I can only fit six dogs at a time in the Mustang. My afternoons are free so I have plenty of time to write.

Mia asked for everyone's attention. "I've made a decision about my future. I've decided to move to California and live with Mum and Julia."

Dad captured Julia's and my looks of shock and disbelief

on his digital camera. Mum broke the stunned silence. "You know I think I'll move here as well. You could build an extra bedroom for me at the back of the house." Mum chuckled. "Just messing with your minds, girls. Just messing with your minds."

Merry Christmas from Claire (*right*), Julia, and Muttley